PRENTICE-HALL
CONTEMPORARY PERSPECTIVES IN MUSIC EDUCATION SERIES
Charles Leonhard, Editor

Bennett Reimer
A PHILOSOPHY OF MUSIC EDUCATION

Robert Sidnell
BUILDING INSTRUCTIONAL PROGRAMS IN MUSIC EDUCATION

Charles Leonhard
THE ROLE OF METHOD IN MUSIC EDUCATION

Edwin Gordon
THE PSYCHOLOGY OF MUSIC TEACHING

Robert H. Klottman
ADMINISTRATION
The Dynamics of Change in Music Education

Richard Colwell
THE EVALUATION OF MUSIC TEACHING AND LEARNING

Clifford K. Madsen and Charles H. Madsen, Jr.
EXPERIMENTAL RESEARCH IN MUSIC

David L. Wilmot
IMPROVING INSTRUCTION IN MUSIC EDUCATION

PRENTICE-HALL INTERNATIONAL, INC., London
PRENTICE-HALL OF AUSTRALIA, PTY. LTD., Sydney
PRENTICE-HALL OF CANADA, LTD., Toronto
PRENTICE-HALL OF INDIA PRIVATE LTD., New Delhi
PRENTICE-HALL OF JAPAN, INC., Tokyo

experimental research in music

CLIFFORD K. MADSEN
School of Music, The Florida State University

CHARLES H. MADSEN, JR.
Department of Psychology, The Florida State University

PRENTICE-HALL, INC., Englewood Cliffs, New Jersey

Music

foreword

Contemporary Perspectives in Music Education is a new series of professional books for music education. It establishes a pattern for music teacher education based on the areas of knowledge and processes involved in music education rather than on the levels and specializations in music education.

The areas of knowledge include philosophy of music education, psychology of music teaching, and research methods. The processes include program development, instruction, administration, supervision, and evaluation.

The basic premise of the series is that mastery of all of these processes and areas of knowledge is essential for the successful music educator regardless of his area of specialization and the level at which he teaches. The series presents in a systematic fashion information and concepts basic to a unified music education profession.

All of the books in the series have been designed and written for use in the undergraduate program of music teacher education. The pattern of the series is both systematic and flexible. It permits music education instructors at the college level to select one or more of the books as texts on the basis of their relevance to a particular course.

In their book, *Experimental Research in Music,* Professor Clifford Madsen and Professor Charles Madsen treat the concepts and techniques basic to experimental research. Their book is remarkable not only for its clarity and comprehensiveness but also for its refreshing and highly readable style.

I shall never forget the occasion of my first reading of this book in manuscript. Having grown accustomed to treatises on research being dull and pedantic, I was amazed and delighted to find myself reading a book on research that was interesting, witty, and down-to-earth, but at the same time filled with information and insights for the beginning researcher in music. There was not the slightest doubt in my mind that this book belonged in Contemporary Perspectives in Music Education.

Music educators are becoming increasingly aware of the necessity for research in music education and the importance of using research and research results in the teaching of music. This book will make a real contribution to a higher level of professionalism in music education which can only be achieved by research oriented teachers of music.

Charles Leonhard

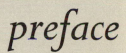

preface

This text is written for advanced undergraduate and graduate students in music who have not had previous instruction in experimental research. Initially, scientific interest is best nurtured by actual experimentation. Therefore, the text is deliberately concise and may be completed concurrently with experimentation. It is written in two parts which may be studied sequentially or by alternating the two sections combining Chapters One and Six, Two and Seven, Three and Eight, Four and Nine, and Five and Ten. The text is primarily intended for a first course in Experimental Research in Music. It may also be used as supplementary reading for courses in Psychology of Music, Music Education, Music Therapy, or Research Methods in Music.

Many musicians recognize the advisability of conducting experimental research but do not know how to get started. The authors contend that students in music should have the opportunity *to begin* experimental research regardless of scientific naivete. In Part One, broad classifications of music topics are presented to stimulate research interest. In Part Two, experimental terminology, rationale, and methodology are introduced. The text is neither a current review of experimentation in music nor a substitute for specific courses in statistics and experimental design. It is the authors' hope that this introduction will provide an impetus for additional experimental research in music.

C.K.M. / C.H.M.

contents

CHAPTER SEVEN

the experimental process   *56*

CHAPTER EIGHT

statistical theory and musicians   *66*

CHAPTER NINE

elementary statistical tests   *77*

CHAPTER TEN

completion of an experiment   *87*

APPENDIX A

selected periodicals   *94*

PART ONE

CHAPTER ONE

music as an art and a science

Many of man's difficulties seem to arise from his naiveté in grouping together aspects of life that are mutually exclusive, and alternately, his inability to distinguish situations and ideas that are necessarily "either-or." [1] Traditionally, most musicians have been in the latter grouping. Even at present, there appears to be a large chasm between musicians interested in more objective approaches to music and those who appear to believe that music as an art would suffer if subjected to scientific scrutiny.

Although this dichotomy is partially justified, it represents an anachronism and may eventually prepare the demise of music as a live art. One need only reflect for a moment on the many accomplishments in the physical and social sciences, as well as on the more commonplace advancements of our present technological age, to realize the limitations imposed by restricting the study of music solely to private studios and the inspiration elicited from great composers, teachers, and conductors. The prac-

---

[1] The concept of "either-or" permeates the text. In scientific research, it is imperative that the student distinguish between factors that are separate and/or dependent. This concept will become more understandable as the student progresses through the text.

tical and artistic fulfillments of other areas of endeavor have not been nearly so limited by this "either-or" dilemma as have those of music.

THE ART OF MUSIC

The pursuit of aesthetic experiences would appear to be not only the first but also the highest endeavor of which man is capable. It is extremely discouraging to find that those primarily concerned with aesthetic endeavors fail to realize that most scientists share this concern. The scientist is also a dreamer (a Romantic, as it were), whose concern is a more complete actualization of man's potentials.

There are many similarities between the scientist and aesthetician. A scientist starts with a hypothesis, euphemistically, a dream. Over a period of time, he develops and builds upon his hypothesis with a goal toward the beautiful. However, all aspects of scientific endeavor demand a paramount necessity for objectification. The scientist's mode of inquiry is based upon structure and rigorous empirical investigation. It is not that he is unconcerned with beauty. Beauty comes from achieving greater specific knowledge. Beauty resides within stringent methodology. Beauty comes from the excitement of each new discovery. Indeed, ultimate beauty seems identical for both science and aesthetics—those endeavors which represent the optimum of which the entire resourcefulness of man is capable.

THE SCIENTIFIC ATTITUDE

Surprisingly, most musicians have only vague ideas concerning research and the place it could have in the music profession. Many musicians believe that research, although respectable, has no real meaning for anyone except esoteric experimenters who lose themselves in inconspicuous laboratories and experiment with musical effects on everything except those aspects that could really benefit the music profession. This attitude may be partially correct, but it is so limited in describing research that it fails to see most of the important aspects of this potentially powerful endeavor.

Research, in the broadest definition, is a way of thinking, a state of mind. It is an attempt to think rationally and objectively concerning those aspects of life that can be studied scientifically. It is a rigorous discipline that attempts to separate fact from fantasy and to test observations in light of objective evidence. This attitude is not necessarily limited to a controlled experiment, which tests specific variables; it also has a parallel in the positive objective thinking that many people use in daily life. For example, the thinking of a student who seriously considers the possibility of death on the highway when traveling hundreds of miles to get home, the thinking that stimulates regular medical attention, or the thinking related to choice of professional occupation. Many who have worked with wayward friends, maladjusted children, or mental patients immediately recognize the *unobjective thinking* that brings many of these people to the therapist's door. A primary concern of therapist, teacher, or friend is to avoid perpetuating the misdirected and misguided thought processes that incapacitate and cause premature death. The research attitude represents an objective view of the world, and the finished product, hopefully, is a person who is informed and has the ability to think, that is, to analyze, to criticize, and to choose alternatives in the light of all possible evidence.

Research is a *modus operandi,* a method by which men can organize actions to be consistent with their thoughts and test these actions intelligently, realizing that through thoughtful trial and error they can better ascertain the worth of their ideas. Most criminal courts evidence tremendous leniency following first offenses, but improved behavior and some understanding about the "hot stove" are assumed after the first "burn."

Research is a manner of evaluation. When making a choice is imperative and action has been taken, the thoughtful person evaluates that action to determine how prior choices affect future eventualities. It does appear strange that even after having been "burned," one often respeats previous mistakes usually assuring similar unfortunate outcomes. Often, there is a misapprehension that if one knows the consequences of an action, he will *not* choose unwisely; but anyone who has received a second traffic ticket, eaten too much every Thanksgiving, or procrastinated studying until the end of every term attests to the fallibility of man. To recognize this fallibility and suspect those desires that clothe themselves in the respectability of thought is perhaps the first step toward the scientific attitude, especially concerning evaluation of previous experiences.

Thus, the research attitude is characterized by three general aspects: (1) an objective state of mind, (2) a structured mode of action, and (3) evaluation for future action. In dealing with the arts, research is sometimes defined very broadly to include creativity and other more subtle aspects not generally associated with objective facts. Regardless, it should be remembered that research does not establish absolutes. It develops explanations and predictions that hold until further investigations provide greater information. Scientific inquiry represents a process toward "truth" relative to man's depth of understanding.

QUESTIONING TRADITION

Music is necessarily a live art, and quality performance continues to prevail. It seems progressively more difficult however, to attract the musical potentialities required for continued artistic excellence. In some instances, the time required to achieve musical finesse seems prohibitive; additionally, many potential performers are lost to other areas.

Musicians basically use traditional approaches that have been passed down through the ages. There are inherent advantages to apprenticeship systems, but they leave little opportunity for speed and efficiency and are definitely out of step with the demands of modern-day instruction. Possibly, the most significant reason for the exclusive perpetuation of these traditional approaches is the conspicuous lack of valid experimental research in applied music. Surprisingly, even though some efforts are being made in this area, some performers seem reluctant to avail themselves of the new ideas and knowledge incorporated in the findings of experimental research. Some performing musicians seem to be unconcerned with anything that cannot be passed on in the privacy of the studio. Many articles, methods, and demonstration-lectures produce little more than personal "testimonials" concerning how music should be performed.

The novice is perplexed and often discouraged in trying to arrive at tangible answers for improving performance skills. A young performer often finds himself in a situation which tacitly demands that he function in an intangible world of pet phrases and unproven suppositions. He is sometimes led to believe that to learn music he must find the right teacher, lose himself in a particular cult, and be implicitly faithful. This student may come to realize that it does not seem to matter how long he has studied or with whom. Each encounter with a new teacher usually demands that, in order to be initiated into the teacher's method, the student substantially reject much of his past learning. The aspiring performer then takes one more step in a never-ending process of tearing down one method in order to replace it with another. If thoughtful, he may realize after many years that for the best performer in the world, the pattern would possibly be the same. The performer might still leave this new teacher's studio with the teacher smiling at him condescendingly saying, "Son, it's good you got here in time. Work hard and do as I say and I will correct all those bad habits, and you will perform correctly."

The tremendous facility required for professional performance demands optimum speed. Much time is wasted when conflicting opinions, which could be tested experimentally, are argued and debated. It would appear that if live musical performance is to continue, other than in highly specialized recording groups, something needs to be done to help bring methodology and artistic attitude more into the twentieth century. This does not imply that Leopold Mozart was not a good instructor for young Wolfgang; he obviously was. It does seem unfortunate, however, that some applied musicians continue *not* to recognize anything outside of "apprenticeship" in the study of applied music, and most aspiring musicians are not Mozarts. Many problems encountered in learning performance skills can be studied scientifically. Does differential music training produce recognizably different results? What should be the optimum temporal relationship between individual, group, apprenticed, or other modes of music instruction? What can programmed instruction, aural, visual, tactile, or combinations of these and other stimuli contribute to music learning? Can psycho-motor skills be increased by extrinsic physiological manipulation before physical patterns are established? Is there a relationship between specific isometric-isotonic exercises and musical performance? What are the effects of various presentations of music literature and/or methodology on student motivation? It would seem that while expertise in teaching is invaluable, it need not be exclusive.

Musicians in institutions of higher learning to whom the responsibility of formal music study has been entrusted have consistently moved toward greater objectification in the instruction of music. The entire history of music education represents a dynamic expansion of music opportunities and improved methodology for increased numbers of students. However, the general tenor of even some of the best institutions still evidences great pressures from the past: the tacit assumption prevails that the best, if not the only, way to study music is to apprentice with a master. This attitude in its *extreme* seems to be based on three assumptions: (1) rejection of another teacher's worth, (2) religious dedication to one's one abstract ideas and methods (which possibly would change if tested experimentally), and (3) a firm belief that any student who does not produce from this inspired teaching is obviously untalented.

Certainly, the above attitudes are extreme and should find little expression in modern institutions. A narrow traditional approach to teaching leaves much to be desired, and often the simplest facts are overlooked. While many musicians spend their lives teaching neuro-muscular skills, some do not attempt to gain an understanding of basic physiology. For instance, many musicians teach their own particular concept of "diaphragmatic breathing" without having a firm knowledge of the human anatomy. This is just one area where extant misconceptions are perpetuated by well-meaning teachers of music who rely on traditional approaches rather than objective evidence. Therefore, many ideas and techniques that can be studied scientifically are still debated, espoused, and indoctrinated by various factions of the teaching profession. On the other hand, researchers within universities are becoming increasingly aware of the vast possibilities of experimental research. New ways are constantly being found to shorten the time it takes to master notation, improve intonation, and increase perception and discrimination, to name but a few of the myriad topics under investigation.

For example, experiments in the area of intonation demonstrate a misleading aspect of strictly personal evaluation. A teacher may believe that a student has a tendency to sing out of tune in a specific situation and may tell him to remedy this tendency. The intonational deviation may be just the opposite of that observed by the teacher, but calling attention to intonation changes the performance regardless of what is said about the direction of the deviation.[2] The teacher may associate improved intonation with his definition of the intonational difficulty and believes that his definition was correct. He does not realize that perhaps *anything* he might have said about intonation would probably have influenced the performance. The teacher may then espouse the generality that students tend to go out of tune in a particular situation. If he is particularly influential, some faction of the music profession may incorporate an "absolute principle." This information combines with other "absolute principles," which are often antithetical, and helps contribute to the "great debates" in music. If the teacher were to test the effects of verbal conditioning upon intonation (using a well-constructed design with adequate controls), then the findings could contribute in a more positive manner to future performances.[3] This knowledge would provide a greater contribution to the profession. It would seem that experimental research holds potential benefits for every music instructor as an augmentation to present teaching effectiveness.

SCIENTIFIC APPLICATION

Music has had practical application for centuries. Literature abounds with examples of the use of music from the earliest times of man to the present.[4] It is apparent that music in various forms and patterns

---

[2] Clifford K. Madsen, "The Effect of Scale Direction on Pitch Acuity in Solo Vocal Performance," *Journal of Research in Music Education*, XIV, No. 4 (Winter, 1966).

[3] Donald G. Albert, "The Effect of Differential Rehearsal Techniques on Pitch Acuity," (Master's thesis, Florida State University, August, 1967).

[4] *See* Doris Soibelman, *Therapeutic and Industrial Uses of Music* (New York: Columbia University Press, 1948). E. Thayer Gaston, ed., *Music in Therapy* (New York: The Macmillan Company, 1968). D. M. Schullian and M. Schoen, eds., *Music and Medicine* (New York: Henry Schumann, Inc., 1948). *Music Therapy*, 1951–62 yearbooks of the NAMT (Lawrence, Kansas: The Allen Press). *Journal of Music Therapy* (Lawrence, Kansas: The Allen Press).

has been employed extensively as therapy in most cultures from their inception. Traditionally, music has often been associated with the supernatural. Some present-day writing still attests to this mystical illusion with citations from literature sources portraying the idea that music somehow finds its way into man's "soul" and serves to alleviate and ameliorate his physiological and psychological discomforts.[5] Nevertheless, scientific uses of music are becoming increasingly apparent.

During World War II, a discipline arose that has gained progressive scientific respectability. As the discipline evolved, the National Association for Music Therapy was founded (1950). The NAMT proposes to provide increasing application and research concerning music in therapy. Many mental hospitals presently employ music therapists who represent firm academic backgrounds in music and psychology. Registered music therapists are also employed in other diverse institutional and community settings, and the massive growth of the field would seem to attest to the validity of this embryonic, yet potentially powerful, specialty.[6]

Scientific application of music in therapy demands an objectivity that many musicians are not prepared to accept. The following are typical questions asked by a person who has just heard about the field: "Does music really help make people well?" "Is it really good for people?" The scientist (and, hopefully, the well-trained music therapist) has three possible answers once these questions are more specifically defined—Yes, No, or I don't know. His answer must be based on evidence, not conjecture. If some aspect of music is "good" for someone, then the scientist wants to know if it is also "bad." Specificity is the key. What specific music experience for what specific person in what specific situation, are factors that need to be known. That "patient X participated in the hospital chorus and seemed to enjoy it," has little meaning *per se* for the scientist. Experiments that test the effects of specified music and music activities in the reduction of specific maladaptive behaviors have greater meaning.[7] Also, the scientist may want to test the pejorative as well as the ameliorative effects of music.

The traditional music therapy training programs are associated with

[5] Bessie R. Swanson, *Music in the Education of Children* (2nd ed., Belmont, Calif.: Wadsworth Publishing Company, Inc., 1964), pp. 1–2.

[6] Registration is based upon an established curriculum, which includes a clinical internship of six months. Information concerning music therapy may be obtained by writing to the National Association for Music Therapy, P.O. Box 610, Lawrence, Kansas, 66044.

[7] *See* B. H. Barrett, "Reduction in Rate of Multiple Tics by Free Operant Consequences," in *Case Studies in Behavior Modification*, eds. Leonard P. Ullmann and Leonard Krasner (New York: Holt, Rinehart & Winston, Inc., 1965), pp. 255–63. Clifford K. Madsen *et al.*, "A Behavioral Approach to Music Therapy," *Journal of Music Therapy*, V, No. 3 (September, 1968).

schools of music and evidence pressures toward aesthetic fulfillment.[8] The music therapist generally has strong attitudes about music as a special *positive* force. However, it seems unwise for the practicing therapist to consider himself a music therapist, music educator, applied musician, conductor, and aesthetician all at the same time and at the same level of competency. The research therapist should be primarily concerned with testing the scientific application of music in therapy. Initial discrimination of role definition seems imperative for scientific objectification. Principles which fail to consider that music experiences used as therapy may often be entirely different from music used in other activities will be principles which are vague and non-utilitarian. As music therapy continues to develop into a behavioral science, it must be based on scientific principles demonstrated through research.

CONCLUSION

We live in a nation where research is of prime importance and where constant scientific investigation is being applied to almost all areas of endeavor. Today, children in grade school amaze their elders with new ways of learning mathematics, language proficiencies, and sophisticated facts from the social and physical sciences. All areas of music are proselyting these students in a highly competitive society. The perpetuation of excellent musical performance still demands many years of rigorous practice, as well as the best possible instruction. Music therapy evidences a progressive need to find new and more effective means of ameliorating man's illnesses, and music education has been entrusted with providing research benefits for the entire academic and general public communities. The music profession should dismiss personal prejudices, avail itself of all possible knowledge, support investigation that could prove beneficial, and work in concert to stimulate and evaluate new techniques and materials that can be produced from experimental research.[9]

STUDY QUESTIONS

1. Are there limitations to viewing the study of music as strictly *either* a science *or* an art? Explain.

---

8 Clifford K. Madsen, "A New Music Therapy Curriculum," *Journal of Music Therapy,* II, No. 3 (September, 1965).

9 Parts of this chapter were initially presented in an article, "Experimental Research in Applied Music," by Clifford K. Madsen, *Music Educators Journal,* LI, No. 6 (June–July, 1965).

2. What are three aspects of the scientific attitude, and how are they useful in the study of music?

3. As music therapy continues to develop into a behavioral science, it must be based on scientific principles demonstrated through research. Explain.

4. Assuming more musicians are being graduated from colleges and universities each year and the performance and abilities of these musicians are steadily improving, is research in the area of music education warranted? Explain.

5. Is it possible that music subjected to research could lose its impact as an art? Why?

CHAPTER TWO

methods of research in music

Although the focus of this text is primarily on experimental research, other modes of inquiry are presented to delineate the experimental area. There are four general methods of research in music: (1) philosophical, (2) historical, (3) descriptive, and (4) experimental. It should be stressed that all modes of inquiry may contribute significantly to knowledge. There are those who argue for one mode of investigation perhaps without realizing the varieties of individual issues, physical phenomena, and life experiences. It appears exceedingly narrow to give credence to only one mode of investigation. Certainly, all forms of research are appropriate for the music scholar.

THE PHILOSOPHICAL METHOD

The word philosophy elicits various responses from musicians. Often, it is considered in relation to the most important issues regarding all aspects of music, and conversely, it is sometimes used to refer to ideas and procedures that are "not practical." One often hears the phrase, "I don't have time to think about it, I have too much to do." Those who contrast "philosophical" and "practical" show their lack of understanding. Whether something is "practical" or not is a legitimate question, but only in relationship to other factors that need explicit definition. Terminology that defines "practical" needs to be established before the question can be discussed and issues analyzed. This process of analysis and criticism, then, represents philosophical inquiry.

It would appear that all aspects of music activities need to be logically analyzed and criticized, to be thought and rethought. The foremost question of "Why?" concerning all music activities needs constant investigation. Thoughtful speculation should always precede important decisions. If this is not the case, there will be much foolish research. Richard Colwell states in the *Journal of Research in Music Education:* "It is the responsibility of philosophy to point the direction for research; to identify specific problems; to agree upon meanings of terms and upon both areas and levels of achievement; to locate and give voice to the needs of the profession so that research is done which can be truly beneficial." [1] Important relationships between "what is" and "what ought to be" merit extremely serious appraisal, as does the entire area of knowledge and how one knows anything. There is no substitute for coming directly or vicariously in contact with the most important ideas and positions available. To think without acting may result in loss, but to act without thinking may produce far worse consequences. *Analysis, criticism,* and *speculation* concerning all variables involved in music are imperative.

Analysis refers to searching out implications of assertions, their consistency, and the assumptions involved in a body of theory. Most research topics in music theory may be classified in the analysis category, for example, "Theoretical Analysis of Brahms' Alto Rhapsody." Additionally, music education concepts, techniques, and programs of study all need to be analyzed. *Criticism* refers to precise examination and evaluation of alternatives regarding musical procedures, compositions, or activities. Often, musical works are contrasted by period, composer, or style. Educational theories are sometimes criticized, for example, "The Impact of Montessori on Contemporary Music Education." Many times specific activities relating to interpretation of musical performance are criticized, for example, "Evaluation of Bel Canto Technique." *Speculation* concerns investigation into any aspect of music with a goal toward projections for the future. Most theories regarding aesthetics, art, intuition, music appreciation, attitudes, and values are speculations. It should be noted that many philosophical studies combine all three of

---

1 Richard Colwell, "Music Education and Experimental Research," *Journal of Research in Music Education,* XV, No. 1 (Spring, 1967).

the above procedures in various proportions. Within a historical perspective, musicology is generally considered as the bridge between the philosophical and historical areas and most often involves analysis, criticism, and speculation.

THE HISTORICAL METHOD

The benefits derived from historical research should be obvious. Various forms of historical documentation are necessary if man is to transmit, other than by the spoken word, ideas and artifacts to future generations. Granted that historical evaluation has a bias, that is, it is most often written or perceived by the person in control, may not factually describe a "true event," and contains different "meaning" for everyone, the foremost question remains—what are the alternatives?

Perhaps one of the most unfortunate circumstances concerning man's interpersonal relationships arises from his seeming inability to learn from the past. While records from the past have provided one vehicle enabling technology to develop tremendously, historical documentation has not yet provided much improvement in man's ability to get along with himself and his fellowman (with or without music). A music teacher who would abhor subjecting his students to the physical discomforts he experienced as a child may calmly watch these same pupils suffer detrimental interpersonal relationships within the music ensemble, stating that "each person has to learn for himself." Thus, interpersonal problems seem to remain cyclic for each generation. Hopefully, those engaged in any aspect of historical research, even concerning the coldest facts, will somehow manage to elicit a spark of humanism that will help man *learn* from the past. This would seem especially pertinent in a "humanistic" area such as music.

Historical research in music is valuable in (1) analyzing the past; (2) preserving artifacts (for example, musical manuscripts, instruments); (3) discovering new artifacts; and (4) providing historical information from one specific situation for possible generalization to other areas. Rigorous historical documentation, even if thought to be deservedly inconspicuous, may help stimulate a respect for scholarship. Indeed, if any research project provides this experience, it is worthwhile.

THE DESCRIPTIVE METHOD

Descriptive methods of research enjoy great popularity, especially among researchers within universities. The most common descriptive

method is the *survey,* which is based on one extremely simple premise—
"If you want to know something about a person or a situation, ask."
This method of investigation allows the collection of extensive amounts
of information with the grestest economy of time. *Ex post facto* evaluation and analysis provide valuable information for interpretation for
future action and data useful for *just knowing.* What are a person's
musical values? How much money is spent on music activities in a certain city? How many music activities are there in a particular mental
hospital? What do former students state as being most beneficial in their
curriculum for professional development? From what socio-economic
backgrounds do professional musicians come? Many diverse questions
can be studied through survey techniques.[2]

Some problems encountered by the survey method should be stated.
It would appear that a major drawback is a lack of reciprocity, especially
when ascertaining opinions. Many questionnaires have never been re-
turned because recipients felt that the questionnaire did not provide
enough latitude in responses. The please-answer-yes-or-no direction that
precedes many questionnaires (opinionnaires) discourages the thoughtful
person. Even when the respondent has the option of five, eight, or ten
gradations, *he may not like the questions.* Survey techniques that include
some interaction, that is, interview techniques, help to rectify some of
the objections but usually limit the number of respondents, therefore
limiting the data. Nevertheless, many aspects of music and allied areas
can benefit from survey methods. Survey methods include (1) studies of
existing conditions, (2) comparisons of conditions, and (3) methods of
improving conditions.

Interrelationship studies constitute a sub-class of the descriptive
method and include (1) the case study, (2) causal comparative studies,
and (3) correlational studies. The case study method enjoys extensive
use, particularly in the fields of psychology and music therapy.[3] It rec-
ognizes the uniqueness of situations and circumstances and provides detailed information which usually concerns one subject. There is a growing number of researchers who reject the concept that group human
behaviors or total music behavior involving many subjects can be studied
collectively, combining actions and responses into "averages." Many
behavioral psychologists categorically ignore any attempt to classify any
aspect of group behaviors. These researchers may use extant statistical

---

[2] The survey is still perhaps the most popular method of research used in music
education theses and dissertations. Excellent models for this type of research can
be found in the *Journal of Research in Music Education,* MENC Publication, NEA
Center; Washington, D.C.

[3] Examples of case studies can be found throughout professional literature. See
Appendix A.

tools for evaluation, but it is usually in specific reference to repeated overt behavioral occurrences for each subject; therefore, the individual case study is preferred.[4]

Cases studies may include total volumes devoted to unique patients or even biographies concerning great historical personages. Spitta's work on Bach[5] could certainly be classified as a major case history although this work is most often thought to be historical. The more frequent case studies generally contain information regarding persons neither as famous nor as rich in historical associations, for example, "A Case History of Five 'Dropouts' in a Public School Music Program." Some areas of investigation seem solely appropriate for the case study method where invaluable information is derived from this mode of research.

A second interrelationship method is the causal comparative study, which assesses causative factors by comparisons of different stimuli, subjects, or events. A third method is the correlational study, which does not assess causality but demonstrates significant relationships. (There may be a high correlation between drownings and ice cream sales, but most likely the drownings are not caused by the ice cream.)

Another sub-class of descriptive research is the *developmental study*. This mode of research concerns *growth* and *trend studies*. A growth study may assess the nature and rate of development of a program, an activity, groups, or individuals. A trend analysis is generally predictive and assesses specific aspects of development to clarify specific attributes and demonstrate significant differentiations. Trend and growth studies may be contrasted with historical research. While historical research deals with the past, a trend analysis describes the past in order to help predict the future, for example, "The Effect of Absolute Pitch Training Upon the Children of Schooled Musicians."

THE EXPERIMENTAL METHOD

Areas for experimental research are defined broadly to include any variable of interest for the music student who desires to use this particular methodology (see Chapters Three, Four, and Five). An experiment should be a most exact endeavor, characterized by the most stringent rigor. An experiment is designed to test a certain variable. This variable

---

[4] See Werner K. Honig, *Operant Behavior: Areas of Research and Application* (New York: Appleton-Century-Crofts, 1966).

[5] Philipp Spitta, *Johann Sebastian Bach, His Work and Influence on the Music of Germany (1685–1750)*, trans. Clara Bell and J. A. Fuller-Maitland (3 vols.; New York: Dover Publications, Inc., 1951).

must be isolated through definition or structure of a precise design and accurately measured insuring validity and reliability. An experiment is *valid* when it measures what it purports to measure. It is *reliable* when repeated measures yield similar results. The value of experimental research resides chiefly with the exactness of the specific knowledge that accrues from this mode of inquiry. Cause and effect relationships are established by isolating the experimental variable and manipulating certain other factors under highly controlled conditions to ascertain how and why a particular event occurs. The measurement of the variable depends upon precise independent manipulation. The *dependent variable* is measured data itself; the *independent variable(s)* are those controlled manipulations structured to produce the data.

Value judgments are both worthwhile and necessary, but a carefully designed experiment may provide far greater empirical evidence for causal relationships. Students may be aware of experimental research underlying the fields of medicine and the physical sciences, but the behavioral sciences and aesthetics have not been investigated through experimental manipulation to the degree evidenced in other areas. However, researchers have recently become increasingly aware of the value of experimentation within the behavioral sciences, and many areas of the humanities are also being quickly assimilated into the mainstream of scientific research.

The following chart represents different methods of investigation.

METHODS OF RESEARCH

I. Philosophical
> A. Analysis
> B. Criticism
> C. Speculation

II. Historical
> A. Documentary
> B. Artifacts

III. Descriptive
> A. Survey
>   1. existing conditions
>   2. comparisons of conditions
>   3. method of improving conditions
>
> B. Interrelationship
>   1. case study
>   2. causal comparative study
>   3. correlational study

C. Developmental
    1. growth study
    2. trend study

IV. Experimental
    A. One-sample
    B. Two-sample
    C. Multiple-sample

LIMITATIONS

A point of great confusion to most researchers concerns the differences between facts and value judgments. Some musicians argue value systems, sincerely believing they are arguing facts. In scientific research, a fact is a fact because it has monolithic acceptance or can be empirically verified. That Mozart wrote music is a fact; that Mozart's music is "good" is a value judgment. A value judgment can only be a value judgment if it is *not* a fact. There must be an equal possibility that Mozart's music is "bad" for it to be *judged* as "good." A fact is either-or, a value judgment is not.

Another major difficulty usually encountered by students who become interested in research is their inability to limit an idea to the point where it can be thoroughly investigated. The beginning researcher is sometimes discouraged by the realization that a major research endeavor provides only a minute and perhaps inconspicuous partial answer to a greater concern.

In experimental research, the importance of specificity, delimitation, and control cannot be overemphasized. A student may become tremendously excited about the effects of music on moods. After much work and time-consuming effort, he may arrive at an experimental design that attempts to test one overt physiological response to one sixteen-measure phrase. His previous enthusiasm may wane appreciably. His desire was to find what this great musical experience was all about; he wanted to see if it happened to everyone. With one study, he wanted to find the "answer" to the aesthetic experience. After the youthful fire is pinpointed to the precision of a laser beam, he may be left with an experiment that will take from three to six months to "test the effect of a selected sixteen-measure phrase on the pulse rate of fifty grade school musicians."

Unfortunately, many students yield to their original romantic desire and, encouraged by scientific naiveté, actually attempt to test everything simultaneously. Consequently, they may collect vast amounts of data that are useless. Often, a few "statistical tricks" are used to "beef up" the report, and then the report takes its place among similar studies that attempt to answer all questions and therefore answer none.[6] Possibly the worst result of this activity is the time serious researchers spend reviewing this morass, only to reject it because it lacks scientific control and precise investigation scrutiny.

CONCLUSION

There are many methods and techniques available for the researcher in music. All modes of inquiry are necessary and appropriate. Clear thinking and specificity are the keys to research. If the time spent in research is used wisely to illuminate important issues, describe and measure situations accurately, or test specific variables, the field of music will have many fragments of valid knowledge that collectively will provide focus for future action. The serious researcher should initially realize that he has indeed an "either-or" alternative concerning his first investigation. *Either* he can investigate a minute aspect of a larger problem and possibly arrive at clear significant information, *or* he can attempt to solve many problems, confound the issues, and add to extant conjecture.[7]

STUDY QUESTIONS

1. List the principal methods of research and briefly explain the value of each.
2. Why is "practical" inquiry important in music research?
3. Define "artifact" as related to historical research.
4. What are some problems of the survey method?
5. What are "either-or" alternatives with regard to experimental research?

---

[6] When the area of research interest is so large that it includes many diverse variables, experimental investigation should not be used unless issues can be defined; another mode of inquiry would be advisable.

[7] Organization of this chapter was based on a USOE project No. 6-1388, "A Conference on Research in Music Education," Henry L. Cady, Project Director, School of Music, The Ohio State University. Copies of this report may be obtained from ERIC Document Reproduction Center, Bell and Howell Co., 1700 Shaw Ave., Cleveland, Ohio 44112.

CHAPTER THREE

physical and perceptual bases for music experimentation

Music is organized sound and silence in time. Its two basic constituents are sound (pitch) and time (pitch and/or silence in spatial relationships, rhythm). These two aspects with ramifications involving people are the primary areas for experimental investigation. The four major areas of investigation for the researcher in music are: (1) physical bases of music, (2) perceptual bases of music, (3) psychological bases of music, and (4) pedagogical bases of music. A discussion of the physical (acoustical) and perceptual (physiological) aspects of music follows.

PITCH

Pitch refers to that subjective characteristic by which we differentiate musical frequencies. The term frequency, or *cycles per second,* is preferred by the physicists, because frequency is more exact than pitch and can be measured with existing equipment.[1] Recently, the term cps has been

---

1 *See* Appendix D.

replaced by Hz after Heinrich Hertz, the late-nineteenth-century scientist who discovered radio waves. Noise varies from music, in that noise does not have *regular* vibrations (cps–Hz). Regular pulsations, from 1 to approximately 15 per second, are usually perceived as distinct, separate sounds (rhythm),[2] while separate impulses from 15–20 are perceived as pitch.[3] The lower limit of hearing pitch is thought to be approximately 20 Hz, the upper limit 20,000 Hz.[4] Pitch is judged by the listener and, as such, represents a socio-psychological phenomenon.[5] Pitch varies with loudness (intensity), quality (complexity), and duration, and also with the psychological and physiological disposition of the listener.

Myriad experiments regarding pitch have been conducted in fields outside the disciplines of music.[6] Precise equipment and a thorough knowledge of acoustics are necessary for sophisticated experimental research in physics. However, the researcher in music, with a tape recorder and/or a stroboscope can conduct many experiments on perception, discrimination, and reproduction of pitch.[7] Why do very young children seem to have such a highly developed sense of musical pitch compared to other auditory discriminations? Is "relative pitch" indeed relative only because of instruction? Would it be possible to teach extremely young children "absolute pitch" identifications much as they learn colors? Is "tone deafness" physiologically inherent or is it perhaps learned through modeling inferior adult performances? Can pitch be used to enhance other auditory discriminations, such as phonics, words, or reading? What are the possibilities of pitch as stimulus control in eliciting or teaching other associations?

---

2 Frank A. Geldard, *The Human Senses* (New York: John Wiley & Sons, Inc., 1965), pp. 118–19. Carl E. Seashore, *The Psychology of Musical Talent* (Morristown, N.J.: Silver Burdett Company, 1919), p. 37.

3 Geldard, *op. cit.*, pp. 118–19. Seashore, *op. cit.*, p. 37. C.A. Taylor, *The Physics of Musical Sounds* (London: The English Universities Press, 1965), p. 148.

4 Charles A. Culver, *Musical Acoustics* (New York: McGraw-Hill Book Company, 1956), p. 65. Geldard, *op. cit.*, p. 95.

5 Paul R. Farnsworth, *The Social Psychology of Music* (New York: Dryden Press, 1958), p. 2.

6 Richard A. Campbell, "The Adequacy of a Traditional Place in the Perception of Periodicity Pitch" (Doctoral dissertation, State University of Iowa, 1962). Raymond J. Christman, "A Study of Shifts in Phenomental Pitch as a Result of Prolonged Monaural Stimulation" (Doctoral dissertation, The Ohio State University, 1952). Bruce D. Faulds, "The Perception of Pitch in Music" (Doctoral dissertation, Princeton University, 1952). G. B. Henning, "The Effect of 'Aural Harmonics' on Frequency Discrimination," *Journal of the Acoustical Society of America*, XXXVII (1965), 1144–46. A. E. Rowenbeug, "The Effect of Masking Pitch of Periodic Pulses," *Journal of the Acoustical Society of America*, XXXVIII (1965), 747–58.

7 Appendix D.

QUALITY

Each transmitting source has its own unique quality. Each voice is different, musical instruments certainly produce different qualities, and even lawn mowers and car engines have distinguishing characteristics. Quality is that characteristic which differentiates sounds having similar pitch and loudness. The acoustical term for quality (timbre) is *complexity*.

Every musical sound is composed not only of its major distinguishing characteristics (for example, A = 440 Hz), but also of other sounds heard simultaneously. These other sounds are called *overtones* or *partials*. A trumpet tone perceived as a concert C contains not only the frequency necessary for that particular C, but other frequencies whose unique arrangement gives the trumpet its characteristic quality. The amount and relative intensity of the other parts of the trumpet sound make it possible (for most people) to distinguish it from an oboe, violin, or piano.[8]

It is assumed that all musicians are familiar with the "overtone series" or the partials, which in many instances are derived from exact mathematical multiples of the fundamental.

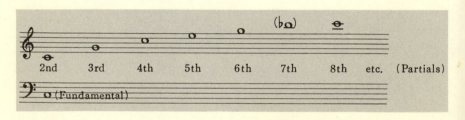

FUNDAMENTAL AND PARTIALS

A pure tone, if indeed it exists, consists of one frequency. A complex tone usually consists of a fundamental (the lowest frequency) and certain other specific frequencies which, when combined, provide distinguishing characteristics referred to as quality.

Many differences in quality that can be detected by electronic equipment escape human differentiation.[9] While extensive laboratory equipment is essential in the investigation of precise tonal analysis, many

---

[8] Culver, *Musical Acoustics*, p. 105. Alexander Wood, *The Physics of Music* (London: Methuen and Co., 1950), pp. 70–77.

[9] J. C. Rissit, "Computer Study of Trumpet Tones," *Journal of the Acoustical Society of America*, XXXVIII, No. 6 (1965), p. 912.

experiments can be conducted empirically to ascertain just what differences in quality are detected by musicians. Previous experimentation in this area demonstrates that, quite often, musicians cannot hear certain differences they believe exist and, conversely, often seem to "hear" much more than can be measured electronically.[10] This seems to be particularly evident in reference to expensive or old instruments or in justification of a certain methodology.

The composite effects of different qualities also need investigation. What sounds are associated with other sensory experiences? What would be the effect on presently constituted musical ensembles of expanding or modifying quality through electronic instrumentation? Is there a "cultural predisposition" toward certain musical qualities? Can pitch and/or quality be used as musical stimuli to effect other behaviors, such as improved speech or hearing?

LOUDNESS

Loudness or intensity is perhaps the most obvious characteristic of sound and warrants extensive experimentation. Intensity is of vital concern to industry, the medical profession, conductors, marching bands, and apparently to many small combos who seem to work on the premise that "If the volume doesn't hurt, forget it."

Some of the questions to be asked in experimentation are these: What intensity is necessary to command attention in music listening? What is the relationship between an original intensity level and selected reproduction levels of the same musical performance? What are the precise intensity levels of individual performers or sections when a musical group is "balanced"? What are the effects of loudness on emotional behaviors? What are the effects of differing noise levels in relationship to learning?

Pitch is to some extent influenced by loudness and should always be controlled in any experimental manipulation.[11] Experimentation could be done on the effects of loudness in relationship to all other musical ingredients. Loudness is measured in decibels (db) and equipment for objective measurement is not exorbitantly expensive (see Appendix D).

DURATION

Duration of sound is often one of the most overlooked and yet vital aspects of music. Experimentation concerning duration of individual

---

10 Farnsworth, *The Social Psychology of Music,* pp. 9–10.

11 Culver, *Musical Acoustics,* p. 84. Geldard, *The Human Senses,* p. 122.

pitches has been conducted,[12] but little investigation has involved the temporal-spatial elements of successive pitches (rhythm). This dearth of research may be caused by the lack of inexpensive precise instruments that can measure rhythmic responses. The development of the Conn Chromatic Stroboscope (Stroboconn) stimulated a great amount of research, probably because of the ease with which individual *pitch* deviations could be measured, but there have not been many investigations concerning rhythm. The several research reports on precise rhythm measurement used specific apparatus usually designed especially for each experiment.[13] Kymograph (time line instruments used for measurements of heart patterns (EKG), of brain waves (EEG), and of muscle potential (EMG) have been available for some time, although many researchers seem reluctant to adapt their use to the measurement of performed rhythms. The development of an *inexpensive* measuring device capable of precise measurement of temporal-spatial impulses should have great heuristic value as a research tool in music experimentation.[14]

Many experiments can be conducted with simple and inexpensive equipment such as an accurate electric metronome, Standard timer (electric clock), and so on. These experiments would not allow the measurement of individual notes, but could establish total temporal deviation over selected rhythm patterns or other variables involving sound in time.

It would appear that consequential contributions to the study of rhythm will initially be those concerned with rhythm in relationship to the physiological limitations and psychological perceptions evidenced in rhythmic "internalization" and rhythmic reproduction (performance). Clichés such as "read ahead" and "sub-divide the beat" might achieve greater meaning when researchers find answers to some basic questions. What is the limit of man's temporal evaluation? (Man obviously cannot tell time as evidenced by the chronoscopes he straps to his arms.) What is a beat? How is a beat measured in music? How slow can a beat occur and still be a beat? How fast? Is all music actually organized or based upon beats, meters, and rhythms? How should beats be sub-divided? Why is the division of twos and multiples of twos (simple) so different

---

[12] C. D. Creelman, "Human Discrimination of Auditory Duration" (Doctoral dissertation, University of Michigan, 1961). K. Danziger, "Effect of Variable Stimulus Intensity on Estimates of Duration," *Perceptual and Motor Skills*, XX (1965), 505–508.

[13] *See* Bernard Linger, "An Experimental Study of Durational Notation" (Doctoral disseration, Florida State University, 1966). Alan H. Drake, "An Experimental Study of Selected Variables in the Performance of Musical Durational Notation," *Journal of Research in Music Education*, XVI, No. 4 (Winter, 1968), 329–38.

[14] S. Fleming, "The Beats Have Found A Master (Tempometer)," *High Fidelity*, XV (April, 1961), 28.

from that of three (compound)? Is it possible for one to sub-divide anything larger than a division of four to *one* beat? [15] What constitutes a scientific definition of rubato and style? How long should a pitch be held within a specific musical context? What determines neuromuscular responses to different temporal stimuli? Why? These are but a few of the many questions open to investigation.

PERCEPTION

Perception of sound has been a subject of serious concern to many diverse investigators representing various disciplines.[16] The ability to hear seems of extreme consequence to everyone in general and to musicians in particular. It is obvious that music must be perceived to exist (with the possible exception of notation, which also necessitates prior hearing if the symbols are to have much meaning).

Researchers in the fields of medicine, physiology, and communication have provided most of the existing knowledge of pitch perception and hearing discrimination.[17] If the perception of minute musical pitch differentiations were as vital to man as his ability to recover a hearing loss, communicate with a loved one, or listen to a ball game, then music researchers would probably become more involved with the perception of sound. Since it is assumed that "everyone can hear music," this pursuit lacks the concern expressed in other fields. There are many questions that may not only prove interesting, but also, when answered, substantially revise current practices regarding music performance, therapy, and education. Preferences in quality, loudness, and certain orchestrations may be solely extensions of physiological perceptional limitations.

[15] Lewis Pankaskie, "Rudiments of Rhythm," Florida State University, Tallahassee, Florida, 1965.

[16] H. G. Birch, I. Belmont, and E. Karp, "Social Differences in Auditory Perception," *Perceptual and Motor Skills*, XX (1965), 861–70. A. E. Brown, "Measurement of Auditory Thresholds," *Journal of the Acoustical Society of America*, XXXVIII (1965), 86–92. G. A. Gescheider, "Resolving of Successive Clicks by the Ears and Skin," *Journal of Experimental Psychology*, LXXI (1966), 378–81. R. G. Petzold, "The Development of Auditory Perception of Musical Sounds by Children in the First Six Grades," *Journal of Research in Music Education*, XI (1963), 21–43.

[17] H. Davis, "Peripheral Coding of Auditory Information," *Sensory Communication* (Cambridge, Mass.: The M.I.T. Press, 1961), pp. 119–41. J. D. Harris, "Loudness Discrimination," *Journal of Speech and Hearing Disorders*, Monograph Supplement, No. 11. G. B. Henning, "Frequency Discrimination of Random Amplitude Tones," *Journal of the Acoustical Society of America*, XXXIX (1966), 336–39. W. D. Neff, "Neural Mechanisms of Auditory Discrimination," *Sensory Communication* (Cambridge, Mass.: The M.I.T. Press, 1961), pp. 259–78.

Musical taste as well as performance difficulties encountered with specific instruments may be directly related to perception.

Experiments testing aural differentiation variables are appropriate topics for investigation. Are there perceptible differences among various brands of instruments? Between the C and D trumpets? Among various models of the same instruments? Between old and new violins? Differentially-priced pianos? Similar melodies? Scale constructs? Different musical styles? Various keys? Many similar questions have indeed been investigated, but there are endless possibilities that remain for the experimental researcher in music.

PHYSIOLOGICAL EFFECTS

The presence of a "deaf" person at a concert, the use of music as an inhibitor of pain, or the conduction of sound through diverse anatomical media attests to the knowledge that music can be felt as well as heard.[18] Perhaps the strong "internalization of the beat" evidenced in dancing and deemed necessary for most musical performance is but another indication that music elicits other tactile responsiveness in addition to the hearing process.

It has been demonstrated that music has the power to modify, to some extent, many physiological processes. Experiments in changes in pulse rate, blood pressure, and respiration as well as "mood" changes measured subjectively and objectively have been reported continuously from as early as 1897.[19]

The subjectivity, inadequate control, and lack of precise measuring instruments cause many of the early investigations to be suspect.[20] The development, both quantitative and qualitative, of precise measuring devices promises expanded research in the physiological area.[21] Also, current bio-chemical research demonstrates physiological changes in behavior that may soon be commonplace in therapy and education.[22] It is

---

[18] Clifford K. Madsen, *et al.*, "The Effect of Sound on the Tactile Threshold of Deaf Subjects," *Journal of Music Therapy*, II, No. 2 (June, 1965), 64–68.

[19] Douglas S. Ellis and Gilbert Brighouse, "Effect of Music on Respiration and Heartbeat," *American Journal of Psychology*, LXV, No. 1 (1952), 39–47. Paul R. Farnsworth, "A Study of the Hevner Adjective List," *Journal of Aesthetics and Art Criticism*, XIII, No. 9 (1954), 97–103. Doris Soibelman, *Therapeutic and Industrial Uses of Music* (New York: Columbia University Press, 1948), pp. 21–81.

[20] *Ibid.*, pp. 21–22.

[21] Appendix D.

[22] Soibelman, *op. cit.*, pp. 82–83. Murray E. Jarvik, "The Psychopharmacological Revolution," *Psychology Today*, CRM Associates, Del Mar, California (May, 1967), pp. 51–59.

extremely difficult, if not impossible, to separate the physiological from the psychological effects of music. It *is* possible to measure overt responses to controlled stimuli to ascertain specific effects in a well-designed experiment. Investigations that report *overt* responses would seem to have greater meaning than speculative conjecture concerning inferred causes.

CONCLUSION

There has been substantial research on the subject of the physical (acoustical) bases of music, but there are many challenges for the researcher interested in pitch, quality, loudness, and duration aspects of sound. The processes of hearing music as well as the effects of music on physiological responses need continued investigation. Textbooks in music theory, fundamentals of music, music for elementary teachers, music appreciation, and so on, are produced in ever-increasing proportions without benefits of experimental research. It would seem that experimental studies could precede and augment current practices.

Again the "either-or" concept should be stressed. It should be apparent that the scientific experimenter can only *deal with the empirical world and measure that which is demonstrable.* The researcher should be content to investigate that which is verifiable and not confuse issues, events, or experiences. Perception and physiological effects are quite different from how one "feels." The world of music is not necessarily an "either-or"; but one does have to know when he is engaged in which mode of inquiry.

STUDY QUESTIONS

1. Define music and discuss its two basic constituents.
2. Compare a "pure tone" to a complex tone and briefly explain the overtone series.
3. List and discuss the four physical components of music.
4. Discuss the statement "Pitch is judged by the listener, and as such represents a psycho-sociological phenomenon." What factors could possibly change pitch perception?
5. List types of experiments that could be conducted dealing with each of the physical, perceptual, and physiological aspects of music.

CHAPTER FOUR

psychological bases for music experimentation

There are many psychological bases for experimental research, but several areas need clarification before the structure of an experiment can be considered. Specificity is still the key, and the researcher must define all issues in order to know precisely which musical variables are appropriate for experimental research.

LANGUAGE ASPECTS OF MUSIC

Music has often been called "a universal language." Whether or not music is indeed a language must depend upon definition. If one supposes reciprocal communication as a defining prerequisite for a language, then certainly music is not a language—much less universal. If one simply means that different types of "music" are evident universally and enjoyed by many, or that music is capable of eliciting differential responses, then music may qualify. The latter definition, however, distorts the concept of language as generally used and attests not to communicative aspects of music, but to the universal and/or specific enjoyment of different types of music. If reciprocity is *not* essential for communication (for example, a textbook where the student cannot ask the author questions), then music may constitute a "non-verbal form of communication." [1]

One basic problem regarding the language aspects of music concerns the intent of the composer. To ask, "What is the composer trying to say?" appears somewhat questionable, for the composer may not know what he is trying to "say" or what specific mood he is trying to create, or he may not be trying to "say" anything.[2] If music is a language, then what does it communicate? Specific words? Concepts? Ideations? Images? Moods? The definition of specific linguistic communication may certainly be stretched to include music, but to what avail? If exact linguistic symbolization is the goal, it would seem wise to leave communication to more accurate and specific models, that is, English, French, Serbo-Croatian, and instead study the effects of music as a "non-verbal form of communication." While music is often used in therapy as an initial contact designed to elicit responsiveness and provide a vehicle for increased verbal behavior,[3] this application of music should not be confused with verbal communication.

Experimentation in the area of learning theory shows that (1) if a person knows what he is supposed to do in a learning situation, (2) and he wants to do it, (3) he probably will.[4] It is possible to program specific associations to music stimuli (for example, the motifs of Wagner), and the indoctrinated musician will "know the correct associations." [5] These learned responses probably enhance the total aural musical experience and certainly are not detrimental. It should be emphasized, however, that specific indoctrinated responses are quite different from a nondescript elusive "power of communication."

There does seem to be justification for music as a powerful behavioral elicitor, especially in proportion to experiential reinforcement.[6] The researcher could possibly add credence to this concept through careful experimentation. Furthermore, the specific area of verbal texts

---

[1] E. Thayer Gaston, "Man and Music," in E. Thayer Gaston (Ed.), *Music in Therapy* (New York: The Macmillan Company, 1968), pp. 7–27. W. W. Sears, "Processes in Music Therapy," in E. Thayer Gaston, *Music in Therapy*, pp. 30–44.

[2] Paul R. Farnsworth, *The Social Psychology of Music* (New York: Dryden Press, 1958), p. 142.

[3] Farnsworth, *op. cit.,* pp. 259–60.

[4] Donald R. Peterson and Perry London, "Behavioral Treatment of A Child's Eliminative Disturbance," *Case Studies in Behavior Modification,* Eds. Leonard P. Ullmann and Leonard Krasner (New York: Holt, Rinehart, & Winston, Inc., 1965), p. 290.

[5] Farnsworth, *The Social Psychology of Music,* pp. 106, 111.

[6] Robert W. Lundin, *An Objective Psychology of Music,* 2nd ed. (New York: Ronald Press, 1967), pp. 172–77.

(for example, opera, art songs, musical comedy) also needs careful research to differentiate the singular and collective effects of text and music. "Communication" may be verified through controlled research when the *effects* of music training and the psychological emotional changes elicited from music and verbal stimuli (affects of music) demonstrate observable behavioral changes. An exact terminological classification needs to be developed to objectify this subjective area before experimentation can begin.

AFFECTS OF MUSIC

Several researchers have studied affective responses to music as evidenced from verbal reports. Lists of adjectives are constructed, music is played, and respondents indicate their "mood." [7] This research represents a commendable effort, but often places the subject in much the same situation as the composer or artist who is compelled to describe his work verbally. It should be considered that there is at least the possibility that artistic and verbal expressions of man may have very little to do with each other. It should also be considered that the questioning process may actually force a subject to conceptualize, visualize, and theorize, when if left alone, he would not. Northrop, in describing the differences between the oriental and occidental cultures gives a rationale for perception of art as "immediately apprehendable" as opposed to "theoretical." [8] The questions "How does it make you feel," "What meaning do you get out of it" are strangely reminiscent of some therapists who constantly interpolate motives in human behavior to justify the elaborate theories that perhaps exist only in their own minds. Nevertheless, there is certainly a great amount of evidence, both scientific and naively empirical, to indicate that music is capable of eliciting differential behavior. Verbal responses as expressions of mood affects need intensive investigation. Research possibilities in this area would seem of vital concern to the music therapist, especially concering "feedback" from patients in ascertaining therapeutic effectiveness.

---

[7] K. Hevner, "Expression in Music; A Discussion of Experimental Studies and Theories," *Psychological Review,* XLIV (1935), 186–204. K. Hevner, "Experimental Studies of the Elements of Expression in Music," *American Journal of Psychiatry,* XLVIII (1936), 246–68. M. Schoen and E. L. Gatewood, Chapters 7 and 8, *The Effects of Music,* Ed. M. Schoen (New York: Harcourt, Brace & World, Inc., 1927).

[8] F. S. C. Northrop, *The Meeting of East and West* (New York: The Macmillan Company, 1960). F. S. C. Northrop, *The Logic of the Sciences and Humanities* (New York: The Macmillan Company, 1948).

MUSICAL TASTE

Individual and collective musical taste have been investigated for years.[9] Unfortunately, most of the concern expressed about musical taste often appears to originate with musicians and educators who seem to be trying to "elevate" the taste of the general public. It also seems more than coincidental that many "researchers" are primarily preoccupied with that music which they believe represents the finest selectivity.[10] It would appear that most people "like" music that has been repeatedly experienced and that they are taught to "like" (that is, music that has been positively reinforced). However, there may be many individual differences of opinion concerning specific composers and individual works. Researchers have gathered vast amounts of data to support general and specific theories of sociological aspects of musical taste. Eminence rankings, enjoyment ratings, counting of recordings, knowledge of composers, space allocations, and program analysis represent areas of investigation.[11] It would appear that musical taste stems from some form of indoctrination in relationship to both social and individual factors. There seem to be pronounced cultural similarities as well as many individual differences.[12]

If there is, indeed, some philosophical justification for music selectiveness, or if there are architectonic justifications for music preferences, these also should be investigated. However, the appropriate mode of inquiry might not be experimental investigation. There seem to be two aspects of taste that may be studied objectively: (1) status quo studies to determine exactly what constitutes taste, and (2) experimental studies designed to test the effects of learning on taste. Both of these areas need terminological classification and objective sampling methods. The sociological area is generally well-suited to descriptive research; longitudinal studies where subjects or music experiences are manipulated or rotated over long periods of time may be investigated experimentally.

MUSICAL ABILITIES

Various researchers have developed myriad tests to evaluate *musical abilities*, for example, aptitude, appreciation, discrimination, perfor-

---

9 John H. Mueller, "The Social Nature of Music Taste," *Journal of Research in Music Education*, IV, No. 2 (Fall, 1956), 120.

10 Farnsworth, *The Social Psychology of Music*, p. 136.

11 Farnsworth, *op. cit.*, pp. 116–77. Lundin, *An Objective Psychology of Music*, pp. 179–89.

12 Farnsworth, *op. cit.*, pp. 152–53.

mance, and so on.[13] The early work of Seashore represents a significant contribution in this area.[14] Other researchers have developed the area in greater detail and specificity.[15] The tests, however, have not enjoyed the use and respect that many initially thought they would have. Many students probably go through music experiences, from elementary school through graduate study, without ever taking any of these tests. Perhaps, ways could be found to make better use of these instruments in the selection and evaluation of music experiences. However, there are those who question the purpose of any such testing and ask, "Why have such tests? How can they be used? Are the tests indeed productive in any way? [16] While extensive work has been done to test the tests and also to correlate them with other attributes, such as intelligence, socio-economic background, achievement,[17] and so on, much remains to be done in this area.

It would seem that the music researcher should also be concerned about the lack of valid and reliable live performance tests. The few rare exceptions in this void, for example, "Watkins-Farnum Performance Scale,"[18] provide the only assessment of actual performance. For some time it has been evident that paper and pencil studies provide only partial answers to performing variables. It is one thing to be able to discriminate subtle differences between two very similar tones; it is quite

---

[13] William E. Whybrew, *Measurement and Evaluation in Music* (Dubuque, Iowa: William C. Brown Co., 1962), pp. 6–7. Paul R. Lehman, *Tests and Measurements in Music* (Englewood Cliffs, N.J.: Prentice-Hall, Inc., 1968).

[14] Carl E. Seashore, *Psychology of Music* (New York: McGraw-Hill Book Company, 1938).

[15] Edwin Gordon, *Musical Aptitude Profile* (Boston: Houghton-Mifflin Company, 1965). H. D. Wing, "A Revision of the Wing Musical Aptitude Test," *Journal of Research in Music Education,* X (Spring, 1962), 39–46. Lehman, *Tests and Measurements in Music* (Englewood Cliffs, N.J.: Prentice-Hall, Inc., 1968).

[16] Whybrew, *op. cit.*, p. 5.

[17] Edward L. Rainbow, "A Pilot Study to Investigate the Constructs of Musical Aptitude," *Journal of Research in Music Education,* XIII, No. 1 (Spring, 1965), p. 3. Clarence E. Garder, "Characteristics of Outstanding High School Musicians," *Journal of Research in Music Education,* III (1955), 11–20. W. S. Graves, "Factors Associated with Children's Taking Music Lessons, Including Some Parent-Child Relationships," *Pedagogical Seminary,* LXX (1947), 65–125. Leta S. Hollingworth, "Music Sensitivity of Children Who Test Above 135 IQ," *Journal of Educational Psychology,* XVII (1962), 95–109, Jo Ann M. Hughes, "59 Case Studies of the Effect of Music Participation on Social Development," *Music Educators Journal,* XLI (February, 1954), 58–59. J. L. Mursell, *The Psychology of Music* (New York: W. W. Norton & Company, Inc., 1937). Hazel M. Stanton, "Measurement of Musical Talent: The Eastman Experiment," *University of Iowa Studies in the Psychology of Music,* II (1935), 1–140.

[18] J. G. Watkins and S. E. Farnum, *The Watkins-Farnum Performance Scale* (Winona, Mich.: Leonard Music, 1962).

different to be able to perform on an instrument with this same degree of subtlety.[19]

Perhaps after many years of basic experimentation in all areas of music, adequate performance tests can be constructed. Someday, sophisticated instrumentation may make it possible for a student to perform before a machine that will quickly assess many variables of performances simultaneously (for example, intonation, timbre, rhythmic stability, subtle nuances) and provide a print-out sheet with exact data expressed in easily-understood terminology. This is certainly within the grasp of our highly specialized technology, but it necessitates an exact classification system followed by research. Statements such as "Blow through the notes," "Support the upper notes," and "Taper the end of the phrase" will have to be modified into more precise terminology that can be experimentally tested. Of course, some musicians will object to such a mechanical device, but the question still remains: What are the alternatives? Such an instrument could serve as a teaching aid as well as a prognostic tool. Over the years, "norms" could be established for different levels of development, and perhaps then the profession could incorporate many of the benefits initially predicted for tests concerning music abilities.

MUSIC IN THERAPY

Stereotypes are extremely common and perhaps no one knows this better than the music therapist. It is difficult, if not impossible, to explain to the layman "What is a music therapist?" and "What is his work?" Most people have several misconceptions of music therapy, and often it is as difficult to explain music therapy as it is to convince a layman that all psychotherapists do not have beards and practice some deep dark ritual over a patient lying on a couch. Surprisingly some music therapists evidence stereotyped thinking concerning the value of research and portray the attitude that while experimental research is respectable, it often has little "practical" value.

The music therapist should be eager to seek scientifically-based procedures and should constantly strive toward greater objectivity. The very nature of the music therapist's work demands a particular objectivity which is essential. If the therapist is not objective in interpersonal relationships, he cannot survive in the therapeutic situation and will

---

[19] Frederick W. Vorce, Jr., "The Effect of Simultaneous Stimulus on Vocal Pitch Accuracy" (Doctoral dissertation, Florida State University, 1964).

cease to function.[20] However, concerning research as a mode of action, evaluation, and prognostication, the music therapist needs much more knowledge. There are many questions concerning the scientific practice of music therapy that should be investigated: Are accurate records kept of music activities prescribed for patients? Precisely how much time does a patient spend in music activities? How is it decided that a patient should engage in a music activity? Which is better, group participation or individual participation? How is improvement evaluated for each patient? What types of music activities should be available? What are the relative benefits of differing music activities? On what basis does the therapist change a patient's therapy program? Is fine musical performance better than activity therapy? and so on.[21]

Many of these questions could presently be answered by the music therapist. However, answers such as, "Well, it depends," or "I believe the patient should have a chance to express himself," or "We try to help those individuals who show they can benefit most from the music experiences" do not constitute scientific justification. If answers are to contribute to the establishment of rapport, the promotion of socialization, and so on, then these terms should be defined in regard to specific overt behaviors and positive amelioration for each patient. For example, if music is indeed "a socializing agent," then operational definition seems prerequisite to subsequent testing. To state that patients singing side by side are "socializing" is somewhat misleading; to equate this "socializing" with a public community choir and a professional orchestra might be irrelevant; and to assume that this "socializing" is monolithically good appears extremely questionable. To place a patient in the hospital chorus for specific reasons pertaining to his particular malady appears wise. If the reason the patient was institutionalized was in part that he could not sing songs side by side with other people, then the speculative positive benefits from this experience seem advisable. Perhaps a patient cannot even approximate any societal interaction except through group music activities. In this case, benefits that might accrue, especially pertaining to stimulus generalization, are obvious.[22] To consider just the

[20] Ardo M. Wrobel, "Roles of the Music Therapist in the Open Institution," in *Music Therapy,* ed. Erwjn H. Schneider, National Association for Music Therapy (Lawrence, Kansas: The Allen Press, 1963), p. 48.

[21] Some of these questions were raised by Donald E. Michel in a descriptive study reported in NAMT *Music Therapy* (Lawrence, Kansas: The Allen Press, 1959), pp. 137–52.

[22] Sally H. Baird, "Some Clinical Uses of Music with Geriatric Patients: A Case Report," in *Music Therapy,* ed. E. Thayer Gaston (New York: The Macmillan Company, 1968), pp. 289–90.

wonderful experience of being in a musical group for all the socializing benefits seems naive.

The field of music therapy has moved a long way toward greater scientific respectability since its inception. Many problems will continue to present challenges to the research therapist. It would appear advisable for the aspiring therapist to gain as much research skill as possible.

MUSIC IN INDUSTRY

There are two areas for research that should be mentioned in a discussion of music in industry: (1) the use of music in industry including the various means by which production or some aspect of a particular skill are involved; and (2) music as an industry. The latter includes the many elements by which music activities can be identified as commercial activities.

Music in industry has been used in connection with a multitude of commodities, skills, and attitude enhancements.[23] Muzak [24] has enjoyed a growing clientele for a number of years, and many diverse institutions, professional offices, and commercial retail stores evidence the use of music. Research needs to be done in this entire area by competent investigators. It is difficult to believe that music would be as prevalent in commercial use as it is without the careful industrial research that definitely demonstrates "business is better," "production is greater," or "workers' attitudes are improved" because of music. However, basic projects need to be carried out that delve deeper into the problems and future possibilities concerning music in industry. Many questions should be asked regarding just what specific effects music has upon shoppers, factory workers, and production rates. What relationships exist between these aspects and music education, music therapy, and music performance? Does the constant bombardment of sound to which most people are continuously subjected increase musical discrimination? Does it help negate cortical responsiveness? Does it contribute to decreased activity, increased activity? Specific questions in this area might lead to research that would not only benefit industry but perhaps have far greater implications for education, therapy, and music performance.

Music as an industry raises questions regarding the "business of music." Academic researchers are sometimes noted for concern about

---

[23] Lundin, *An Objective Psychology of Music,* pp. 291–304.
[24] *Ibid.,* pp. 294–95.

traditional "Master Works," [25] but the actual or partial *control* of most of the nation's music activities may be substantially apart from anything that is currently being investigated. Records, music instrument sales, participant activities, radio, TV, movie scores, and all other commercial aspects of music need more intensive investigation, and results made available.

Unfortunately, "popular music" or "commercial pursuits" often appear to lie outside the proper province of serious academic researchers. While studies are conducted to determine the need for musicians to teach and engage in music as a financially remunerative *profession*,[26] there appears to be a dearth of investigation concerning "music and money." It may be a rather tainted subject, but it may provide key answers directly relating to other areas of more immediate concern to the profession. It appears unwise not to recognize the many financial aspects of music as a business and the popular music that is being employed by the vast majority of people in the nation.

CONCLUSION

There are many psychological bases for music experimentation. While music has been called "a universal language" as well as a means of "non-verbal communication," the specific nature of this communication needs to be assessed. Music effects people differently, and therefore separate areas of mood affects, musical taste, and musical abilities need extensive experimental investigation toward greater specificity. Research in these areas would be of special interest to music therapists, who need much more specific information concerning the use of music for physiological and psychological amelioration. Research in this area might use current "behavioral methods" to test the effectiveness of music in shaping appropriate adaptive behaviors. The use of music in industry, and allied "professional" considerations, might also be investigated. Implications from these areas should be of concern to music educators and to applied musicians.

Issues should not be confounded for the therapist, performer, or educator. The "either-or" of many diverse music aspects should be initially understood before the investigator proceeds with an experi-

---

[25] Paul R. Farnsworth, "Elite Attitudes in Music as Measured by the Cattell Space Method," *Journal of Research in Music Education*, X, No. 1 (Spring, 1962), 65.

[26] Fred K. Grumley, "A Study of the Supply and Demand for College Level Music Teachers with Doctoral Degrees, 1964–1970" (Doctoral dissertation, Florida State University, 1964).

ment; the researcher should not combine several areas and variables that need to be assessed separately. While implications can be assessed for interpretation in all areas of music, the researcher must isolate specific variables to be tested in reference to any primary area. Language should not be confused with mood; musical abilities should be separated from taste; status quo studies should be separated from the process of music education; and aspects of the affective domain need to be tested by assessing specific music effects.

STUDY QUESTIONS

1. What is the nature of "music communication"?
2. What are factors that contribute to a person's musical taste? How may taste be studied objectively?
3. What are some of the differences in behavior elicited by music and how might they be of interest to the music therapist?
4. What is meant by the phrase "music as a business"?
5. List and discuss several topics concerning the psychological bases of music that seem appropriate for experimental research.

CHAPTER FIVE

pedagogical bases for music experimentation

One of the most consequential aspects of experimental research concerns music education. Although most research in music comes from the theses and dissertations written in partial fulfillment for degrees in graduate schools, a most unfortunate aspect of this research is that it usually stops upon completion of the degree. Just when the student has attained the sophistication to conduct independent research (*after* the completion of a dissertation), he usually stops this particular pursuit, never to continue. Even at the professorial levels there are many who just vaguely remember the design and statistical concepts that they so ardently pursued as graduate students. While some continue to supervise research throughout their professional lives, it would appear that a greater number only remember research as the last hurdle toward the completion of the graduate degree.

Experimental research does not begin to enjoy the respect and popularity it should have in the teaching profession, particularly in relationship to basic research in teaching and learning. As one reviews existing experimental literature, one is often left with the thought that many experimental studies were designed to prove a particular point of view or teaching technique. It has been said that "all educational experiments are doomed to success." Seldom can much real knowledge arise from an investigation determined to prove that which one already "knows." There is a lack of investigation in the most basic issues relating to the teaching-learning situation and the most elementary aspects of music. It is probable that significant progress in these areas will be made in the future.

ATTRIBUTES OF MUSIC

Since many of the most fundamental aspects of music seem to be the most elusive, this chapter deals with the most obvious considerations of music for the teacher, and presents them with foremost simplicity. This is not intended to represent the totality of issues or problems concerning music education.

The first question concerning the music teacher would seem to be, What is music? The next question would concern the attributes of music, that is, What can one do with music? The third question, Can these attributes of music be learned? The fourth, Can they be taught? And lastly, How does one go about teaching them?

Music is organized sound and silence in time. Music can be (1) composed, (2) performed, (3) listened to, (4) verbalized, (5) conceptualized, and (6) used for extra-musical purposes.

COMPOSITION

Music is composed. The process of composition is generally thought of as synonymous with "creativity," although the general category of composition may also include arranging and orchestration. Is creativity simply a reorganization of past experiences, or is it mystical or supernatural, unexplainable in the empirical world? That Mozart wrote occidental music instead or oriental music would seem to support the first point regarding reorganization of past experiences. That Mozart wrote the quality of music he did at such a tender age seems extremely difficult to explain at all.[1]

Questions for teachers concerned with composition and creativity would seem to be, Can creativity be learned and can it be taught? If it can be *taught* but not learned, the pursuit seems irrelevant. If it can be *learned* but not taught, then perhaps the teacher should be concerned

[1] W. J. Turner, *Mozart: The Man and His Work* (New York: Doubleday Company, Inc., 1956).

with the *situation* where this learning can take place. Other questions arise at this point. Can the student create from nothing? If not, what implements and information does he need? If instruction in the use of these tools is given, does progressive instruction inhibit future creativity? These are questions that need to be answered not only by thoughtful teachers concerned with music composition, but also by those concerned with other creative music activities.

Possible answers might lie in the precise point at which instruction in manipulation of specific tools of the art should end and in whether evaluation of a creative work should come from the teacher and/or the student. Experimentation with very young children would seem invaluable in answering some of these questions.[2]

PERFORMANCE

The area of performance appears to be the major concern for many within the teaching profession. Most of what constitutes music education is the teaching and learning of performance skills. The necessary prerequisite for performance is listening, which will be discussed later. *Music performance is an active endeavor, which for the most part consists of perfecting neuro-muscular responses in relationship to judgmental aural discriminations.*

One significant problem encountered in discussing music performance skills is the chasm that has developed regarding neuro-muscular responses and other similar activities. Tightrope artists, football artists, juggling artists, and singing artists have a great deal in common: they develop neuro-muscular skills to an extremely high level. Learning to type and learning to play the piano are somewhat similar pursuits. The analogy is quite obvious in the initial states of developing skill on the two "instruments" and can be carried quite far. Of course, there are differences and these differences are extremely important. Nevertheless, the development of patterns of responses is quite similar for many activities. Many musicians abhor these comparisons. It is an insult to refer to a physician as "a butcher," regardless of how skillfully the physician uses a knife. The distinction, however, concerns societal status, consequences of the act, and many other related issues, not necessarily how adroitly one performs a neuro-muscular skill. For example, it is evident that the human organism must maintain a certain bodily temperature to function

---

2 *See* Gene Simons, "Comparisons of Incipient Music Responses Among Very Young Twins and Singletons," *Journal of Research in Music Education*, XII, No. 3 (Fall, 1964), 212–26.

at peak neuro-muscular effectiveness.[3] Athletes have known this for hundreds of years. They usually "warm up" before engaging in demanding physical pursuits. This warm-up consists of some simple activity to increase bodily functions and generate heat in preparation for performance. The common charley horse is partially caused by the contraction of a cold muscle, and usually a little skin-to-skin rubbing, which generates heat, will relieve the contraction. The entire idea of "warming up" is placed in perspective by most athletes. Contrast this concept with that evident in some music study. The initial concept of physiological preparation is almost completely lost in hundreds of lip slurs, long tones, vocalises, articles, and testimonials, which may have little if any relationship to "warming up." Thus, neuro-muscular preparation is confused with making music. The major point here is not the example. *Music is an aesthetic art, and because it is capable of eliciting intense emotive responsiveness, many teachers confuse the art object* (that is, the finished performance) *with the pedagogical process.* When discrimination between the process and the object is lacking, cultism flourishes.

Performance also necessitates imitation for the development of skills. Most imitative behaviors can be studied scientifically. Experiments can be designed that assess visual, neuro-muscular, and aural elements of performance as well as direct and vicarious modeling effects.[4] For example, conducting necessitates all of the aforementioned imitative behaviors. Again it should be stated that the scientific study of music performance demands analysis and experimental verification in order to know which specific behaviors should be shaped and the best methods by which this can be accomplished. Music as an art has nothing to lose from the application of scientific method. Objectification should not be confused with insensitivity.

LISTENING

Listening to music seems prerequisite to all other musical pursuits. *Discrimination* is the basis for listening. The first level of discriminatory perception is whether music is being heard or not being heard. The point is not so obvious when one considers the many situations where it is difficult to ascertain whether music is really "on" or "off." Background

---

[3] M. Gladys Scott, *Analysis of Human Motion* (New York: Appleton-Century-Crofts, 1963), p. 180.

[4] For information on modeling, *see* Albert Bandura, "Behavioral Modification Through Modeling Procedures," *Research in Behavior Modification,* eds. Leonard Krasner and Leonard P. Ullmann (New York: Holt, Rinehart & Winston, Inc., 1966).

music exists in our culture in large proportions, and most people are conditioned to being "bathed in sound." Listening to music, as far as the educator is concerned, should transcend this "on-off" level and include additional discriminations. An old cliché states that "all of life is like a bath, once one gets used to it, it's not so hot." Perhaps this is especially applicable to music. There seem to be many people who "enjoy" listening to music, but their attention to the music wanes appreciably after the initial stimulus, and they prefer to daydream and "drift with a mood." Hence, there appears to be little concentration on the music. Mood affects are often extremely desirable and especially vital to the music therapist. Mood affects are also very important in music education, but these experiences should not be confused with developing listening skills.

Partial answers to questions concerned with enhancing the listening experience might lie in investigations that attempt to test the effects of different types of successive programs aimed at teaching effective discrimination. One such program might experiment with two pitches contrasting the respective differences of the two sounds. As successive pitches are presented, the elementary concept of introducing form might be investigated. For example, one might start with one pitch and from one pitch go to two, to three, to a group, to a phrase, to a melody, to an embellishment of the same melody (variation form), then to a different melody (binary form), and back to the original melody (ternary form). The melody could be presented to "chase itself" (canon) and to chase itself with the same melody at a different interval (fugue). The simple song forms could be extended to encompass larger forms (sonata, rondo, etc.). This process could provide many experiments concerning the development of discrimination skills.

Another approach could experimentally test effective discrimination programs involving the differentiation of the *composite* sounds of an ensemble. The student could be given *something specific to listen for,* (high-low, loud-soft, fast-slow, short-long) and progress to greater discriminations (for example, tutti-concertino, strings-winds, strings-brass, trumpets-trombones, trumpets-horns, trumpets-trumpets) with the experimenter testing effective discrimination presentations. This approach might gradually encompass subtleties of orchestration with experimental verification. Another program might concentrate on the awareness of specific motifs, both rhythmic and harmonic, testing the subtle discriminations in harmony and style (theoretical analysis).

Listening is one of the most significant aspects of music; therefore, it is important enough to investigate thoroughly. Myriad experiments are awaiting the skillful investigator. The above processes in the programs being tested are conjectural. All variables concerning aural discrimination need to be tested and retested. New approaches await the verification of controlled research. The novice researcher should not be "looking for a topic," he should be delimiting from his vast musical experiences those specific topics that are vital and exciting for experimental research.

VERBALIZATION

Verbalization is of two kinds, oral and written. *Oral* aspects of music have to do with talking about music, and talking represents a very large part of the total time devoted to the study of music. Man's greatest differentiation from other species is this ability of communication—it warrants precise investigation. Most music instruction falls into this category. It would seem that since most teaching involves talking, the various ways teachers talk about music should make a great difference in teaching effectiveness.[5] Many experiments should be conducted that only test the effect of verbal instruction on music performance. To a large degree, talking is the major activity of the music teacher.

Written aspects of music verbalization concern history and terminology (notation, dynamic markings, etc.) Historical aspects of music might seem outside the province of experimental research, but this is not the case. Many experiments can be conducted concerning historical implications for music education. Many of the old concepts of the relatedness of historical perspectives, music performance, composition, and "appreciation" need to be examined. Does the assimilation of historical knowledge really improve performance? How much historical information should accompany basic appreciation courses, elementary school music series, and applied methodology? These are answerable questions once the goals of study are defined and operational definitions are established. (See the section on Historical Research in Chapter Two.)

Written aspects of music include notation as well as all written symbols used for music. These symbols are of extreme importance in the study of music and should be investigated. The thoughtful investigator might pick up a favorite score and ask himself, "If I were forced to eliminate written symbols from this page, what would constitute the finished hierarchy? Should the title go first or perhaps the composer's name? Are the measure lines important, the metronomic markings, the meter signature, the dynamic markings? Where would one stop? Where would one stop and still have something that could be performed? What on the page is helpful? What is necessary?" These questions should pro-

---

[5] *See* Frank A. Edmonson III, "The Effect of Interval Direction on Pitch Acuity in Solo Vocal Performance" (Doctoral dissertation, Florida State University, 1967).

vide many ideas for experimentation. The effects of specific rhythmic notations on performance might provide a lifetime of research; the way rhythms *should* be notated could perhaps fill another.[6]

CONCEPTUALIZING

To *think* about music requires information and is defined as the process one uses to analyze, criticize, and choose alternatives. Music students can be taught to think about music, and obviously all other aspects of music learning are concomitant with these thought processes. Thinking does seem quite difficult. It is much easier to "believe" than to think. Believing is not only easier, it often provides a good way to absolve individual responsibility and, therefore, blame someone else when things go wrong. ("That teacher wrecked my voice." "I'd play horn better now if it were not for my previous teacher." "That is what the tempo mark said! How was I supposed to know he wanted a decrescendo?") Clear thinking and individual responsibility are imperative for the researcher since the research product must stand on its own merit.

The term *conceptualization* is also used to refer to that aspect of intellectualization that concerns aesthetic appreciation. This is an area which needs much careful objective inquiry. Webster lists the Greek *"aisthētikos*—sense perception—to perceive,"[7] in definition of the word aesthetic. This is understandable. Webster continues with "1 a: relating to or dealing with aesthetics or the beautiful; b: artistic. 2: appreciative of, responsive to, or zealous about the beautiful."[8] This too, is understandable, but the "aesthetic experience," which some say represents a somewhat mystical entity, continues to be elusive. Perhaps this "mystical aesthetic experience" represents *the composite emotional and intellectual responsiveness to music which is modified and reinforced through time and always defined as good.* It should be emphasized that the experimental researcher must deal with overt behavioral responses. If aspects of aesthetic appreciation are to be investigated, terminology must be specific and responses demonstrable and measurable.

---

6 *See* Bernard Linger, "An Experimental Study of Durational Notation" (Doctoral dissertation, Florida State University, 1966).

7 *Webster's Seventh New Collegiate Dictionary* (Springfield, Mass.: G. & C. Merriam Company, Publishers, 1963), p. 15.

8 *Ibid.,* p. 15.

EXTRA-MUSICAL ASPECTS OF MUSIC

Extra-musical considerations are defined as all aspects of music encompassing areas outside the art for its own sake. These include music therapy, music in industry, music for dancing, and music used for recreation as well as ·other less specific areas such as music for socialization, cooperation, citizenship, understanding, and the many other positive qualities often attributed to the study of music.[9] How wonderful the world might be if music were capable of so much.

It would appear that transfer of learning is extremely unlikely, unless the teacher specifically teaches for transfer effects.[10] Yet many music teachers continue to justify music activities by alluding to many types of extra-musical benefits that transfer from the music program (for example, cooperation, socialization, moral enhancements). Experimentation would corroborate or reject some of this speculation. While there appears to be some justification for an indirect route to a particular goal, it would seem that if one wishes to learn music, one should study music, not mathematics, dancing, or citizenship. Conversely, if one wishes to study mathematics, dancing, or world understanding, the study of music may prove to be a poor substitute.

While many auxiliary benefits might accrue from music activities, these benefits need to be demonstrated. Even if verified, extra-musical elements may not constitute the raison d'être for music education. This is a question for philosophical inquiry. It would be wiser for the researcher to direct his time toward investigating instruction through carefully-controlled experimentation than to defend the status quo with claims about extra-musical attributes that may inhibit increased acceptability and that, perhaps, do not exist.

CONCLUSION

There appears to be a dearth of expertise in and acceptance of experimental research, perhaps because many professional educators fail to continue formal research after completion of a degree. Investigation needs to be continued in all aspects of the learning and teaching of music.

---

[9] For an evaluation of extra-musical justifications, *see* Charles Leonhard and Robert N. House, *Foundations and Principles of Music* (New York: McGraw-Hill Book Company, 1959), pp. 96–102.

[10] See B. F. Skinner's *Cumulative Record*, rev. ed. (New York: Appleton-Century-Crofts), 1961.

It is unfortunate when teaching and research represent an "either-or."

Music is defined as organized sound and silence in time, and six attributes are evident. Music can be: (1) composed, (2) performed, (3) listened to, (4) verbalized, (5) conceptualized, and (6) used for extramusical purposes. The major questions for the educator are: (1) Can these attributes be learned? (2) Can they be taught? (3) What are the best ways to go about teaching them? Experimental research concerning all of the above seems limitless.

Aesthetic appreciation should continue to reign supreme in the domain of introspective subjectivity, although it is apparent that the researcher can only measure the attributes of the empirical world. If the aesthetic experience is indeed above scientific scrutiny and defies operational definition and subsequent testing, then it would appear wise to leave it with other transcendental experiences and not attempt the impossible task of "proving" the supernatural world by contriving "evidence" from measured reality. It should be remembered that the poet and philosopher have most often foreshadowed the achievements of the inventor and scientist. Theoretical abstraction is certainly a worthy pursuit, but the scientific investigator must always remember in what mode of inquiry he is engaged.

STUDY QUESTIONS

1. What is creativity? Can it be learned? Can it be taught?
2. Discuss the statement, "Music performance is an active endeavor, which for the most part consists of perfecting neuro-muscular responses in relationship to judgmental aural discriminations."
3. What experimentation could be designed to test various levels of listening discrimination?
4. List aspects of music study that concern verbalization. Relate them to the conductor, applied teacher, and elementary music teacher.
5. Define the "aesthetic experience." Can any aspect of your definition be tested?

PART TWO

CHAPTER SIX

quantification in research

For thousands of years man has had difficulty with his environment. Some problems concerned the procurement of food, the threat of a thief, a place to live, and to what extent he could manipulate his surroundings. Some situations were different from others, some seemed the same, but the more he observed, the more things he saw. After some time and with apparent difficulty, he devised a method for general classification—he learned to count.

CLOSED SYSTEMS

Over the years, man has developed many closed systems—arithmetic, geometry, English, German, Arabic, music notation, the overtone series, and statistics to name but a few. The term "closed system" is used to advance the concept that these various systems are often intrinsically consistent; that is, internal relationships are always constant, but extrinsically invalid (closed). The systems are defined as "closed" because they lose intrinsic consistency when applied to each other or to different phenomena. For example, the relationships between the arithmetic numbers 1 to 2 to 3 is always invariate. These three numbers represent the same relationship as do the numbers 2 to 4 to 6. Also, $1 + 2$ always equals 3. A problem arises, however, when this simple arithmetic system is used to quantify other areas, activities, or products. To state that "one apple plus one apple equals two apples" presents only slight difficulty. To state that "one apple plus one kumquat equals two pieces of fruit" is perhaps justified, but to state that "one apple plus one atom plus one universe equals three things" seems rather tenuous. The same difficulty applies to other closed systems. How much Arabic could one learn with an Arabic dictionary if one knew nothing about the symbols or their "meaning." Since every word in a dictionary is nothing more than a "definition" of every other word, one could not even get started without transferable relationships. Music notation has no meaning for a plumber except in relationship to other factors that have been learned through the *transfer* of perceived phenomena; for example, it may be that the plumber sings in church.

Some systems are related, and transfer is easier, for example, English and French with 46 percent cognates, arithmetic and algebra with digits and some symbols in common, the overtone series and some chord structures. Pitch is quantified in terms of frequency and loudness in terms of decibels. However, even with common elements, transfer can still be a problem when moving from one system into another. One of the basic rationales of the now old "New Math" was to avoid the pitfalls of learning one closed system after another. Because of the difficulties encountered when transferring from arithmetic, to algebra, to geometry, to trigonometry, and so on, modern mathematics now teaches most of these various systems *simultaneously,* using the concept of "sets." Quantification (counting, classifying) is considered less tenuous when any well-defined collection of objects (for example, oranges, limes, lemons, tangerines) is thought of as a set.

Questionable as is the process of transferring closed systems and subsequently inferring meaning, it represents a major resourcefulness of man and distinguishes him from other animals. Man's accomplishments in quantification have provided tremendous progress. It is the quantification of specific responses and subsequent logical methods of analysis that provide the background for experimental research.

SCIENCE AS A DEDUCTIVE METHOD

The rules of logical *deduction* are rules for arriving at true consequences from true premises. *Induction* is the process of reasoning from a part to a whole, from particulars to generals. Once a theory or principle has been established, it can be tested deductively, and repeated observations can ascertain its validity. A problem arises for the empirical scientist: how does one go about arriving at the "truth" of the *initial* proposition? Since it is impossible for the scientist to observe all possible situations, he must generalize from what he thinks true of some observations to what is true for all possible observations. This represents a problem of induction, and any empirical science begins with particular observation and subsequent generalization. Mathematical systems such as probability theory are by their very nature *deductive*. Once the experimenter can make assumptions about what is true, then statistical theory based upon probability indicates how likely he is to observe particular results considering the laws of chance. Thus, experimental research combines these two processes; deduction is used to test observed data as a ground for induction.

METHODS FOR EXPERIMENTAL RESEARCH

Specific rationales for experimentation (observation under controlled conditions) were advocated by John Stuart Mill, who analyzed the search for causes in experimental research in order to identify the means by which experimentation may be achieved. These constitute the five Mill's Canons, or rules for experimental research.[1]

1. Mill's *Method of Agreement* proposes that if the circumstances leading up to a given event have in every case only one common factor, that factor probably is the cause. Thus, if through controlled experimentation it could be found that in the vast possibilities of musical experience only one factor could be found in common to some specific attribute (that is, perfect pitch, tone deafness, and so on), that factor would be the cause of the attribute. Many experimental designs using the One-Sample Method approximate this principle when attempting to assess the effect of manipulation of one variable at a time. The limitations of this method are appreciable because of the assumption concerning the *dis*similarities of *all* other factors. It is an extremely tenuous assumption to assess causality on the basis of single rather than multiple variables unless a functional analysis is performed.

2. Mill's *Method of Differences* proposes that if two or more sets of circumstances are alike in every respect except for one factor and if a given result occurs only when that factor is present, the factor in question probably is the cause of that result. It is difficult, if not impossible,

---

[1] John Stuart Mill, *A System of Logic*, Book III, Chapter 8 (New York: Harper and Brothers, 1873).

to create experimental conditions where all sets of circumstances are alike in every respect. Yet, this principle constitutes the major rationale for much experimentation (Equivalent-Sample Method) where individuals are matched, divided into control and experimental groups, and subjected to scientific manipulations, after which differences are assessed.

3. The *Joint Method* combines the above two methods. First, the one factor common to the occurrence is found (Method of Agreement), and second, the factor is withdrawn to determine if the phenomenon occurs *only* when the factor is present. When conditions of both the Method of Agreement and the Method of Differences are satisfactorily met, identification of causes should be reasonably conclusive. Sophisticated experimental designs (techniques alternating individual, group, or variable measures) use the rationale of the Joint Method. Specific factors are isolated and assessed, after which these factors are omitted and/or replaced with subsequent assessment. Often, the process is continued over extended periods with many rotations. The major difficulty in a rotation design is the factor of "learning" (or order effects), which tremendously complicates the assessment of the individual factor (variable) *after the initial rotation.*

4. The *Method of Residues* assesses causes by the process of elimination. This method proposes that when the specific factors causing certain parts of a given phenomenon are known, the remaining parts of the phenomenon must be caused by the remaining factor or factors. This is an uncertain procedure for specific conclusions; yet, it most aptly describes the entire process of *continued experimentation,* where unknown factors are constantly being found and evaluated to explain the additional aspects of a phenomenon.

5. The *Method of Concomitant Variations* proposes, in effect, that when two things consistently change or vary together, either the variations in one are caused by the variations in the other, or both are being affected by some common cause. Often, it is impossible or undesirable to isolate only one factor for study, that is, to conduct an experiment. When this is the case, inferences must be drawn from assessing the relationship among factors (correlation) and taking into account extrinsic variables (growth analysis, trend studies, causal comparative studies).

These five methods of investigation apply to individuals and groups as well as to inanimate objects, which are much more easily controlled. They represent methods by which the experimenter can begin to structure a design appropriate to the investigation of the proposed topic, see chart pp. 84–85.

While experimental design texts do not generally discuss Mill's Canons and apply them to research, the importance of a verbal rationale for those who have had little background in the scientific disciplines is apparent.

DESCRIPTIONS IN MUSIC QUANTIFICATION

Prior to proceeding to elementary principles of experimental design and statistics (Chapters Seven and Eight), a few brief descriptions of separate and related areas of experimental quantification are advisable.

Statistics is the collection and classification of facts on the basis of relative frequency of occurrences as a ground for induction.

Data processing involves the use of computers for any number of diverse computations including classifying and amassing separate data and statistical analysis.

A *computer programmer* is a person who writes a "program" or instructions by which data are analyzed by the computer.

There are many *computer programs* for statistical analysis. Pre-written programs for common statistical tests are available in any university computer center. Thus, a music student may use a pre-written program rather than going through the long process of working out by hand complex statistical formulas.[2]

Experimental design is the process by which scientific experiments are structured to measure a defined variable. This process requires knowledge of the subject area and some knowledge of elementary principles underlying statistics. Experimental design does not require any knowledge of computer usage. However, this knowledge can be extremely helpful in saving time when a pre-written statistical "program" can be used or a new program developed. This is of particular interest in many music experiments where thousands of separate observations regarding individual pitches and rhythms need to be analyzed.

Programmed instruction is a separate area and should not be confused with a "computer program." Programmed instruction usually refers to a process of self-instruction with instantaneous "feedback" (for example, a programmed textbook). Complex programmed instruction (for example, Computer Assisted Instruction) uses a computer for immediate evaluation and appropriate reinforcement of specific responses. This programmed instruction necessitates not only the hardware (computer), but also the software (that is, programs from subject matter specialists)

---

[2] W. J. Dixon, ed, *BMD Biomedical Computer Programs* (Los Angeles: University of California Press, 1967).

for its actualization. Writing a programmed text requires knowledge of the subject matter area and principles of programming. If any instructional program is to be tested in comparison to other instructional media, then knowledge of experimental design and statistics is necessary for valid comparisons and interpretation.

Specifically different from any of the above is *computer music.* Music that is actually written (programmed) for, and/or performed by, a computer.

Competency in any of the above areas demands strenuous preparation; it is rare indeed to find a person well qualified in all.

LIMITATIONS OF QUANTIFICATION

It is purported that Disraeli once said, "There are three kinds of lies: lies, damn lies, and statistics." When the student views a television commercial and is told that four dentists out of five recommend a certain mouthwash, that might actually be the case—the total number of dentists equals five. Or perhaps after interviewing 800 dentists in groups of five, the company found 4 and only 4, out of one group of 5 that would recommend the product. A student can be the "highest in the class" and not be able to find either side of his desk with both hands. Alternately, a student may be in the "lowest part of the class" and demonstrate a firm command of the subject matter. If only partial information is given, "numerical tricks" can be deceptive.

It also appears that some people who work with numbers over an extended period of time come to "believe them." Most students have had the experience of questioning the basis on which their grade was given. The student may find himself looking over numbers in a roll book as though the roll book numbers were responsible for his grade. Each instructor usually chooses the text, determines the content of the course, constructs the tests, decides what responses are "right or wrong" and their relative weighting, and decides how much individual tests and assignments will count toward determining the final grade. For the teacher to then view *his* amassed numbers as though they had some extrinsic absolute worth may represent a case where "numbers are believed." It should be stated that most teachers use many statistical concepts to assess a student's work and arrive at individual grades with as much objectivity and genuine fairness as possible.

It must be remembered that application of numbers or mathematical systems per se do not necessarily establish "truth." Even if four dentists out of every five recommend a mouthwash, this does not tell much about the mouthwash or firmly establish that it is "good." The value and meaning of products, circumstances, situations, and all aspects of phenomena are always open to interpretation. While it would be unwise to jump off a building hoping to discount the laws of gravity, to assume dental expertise without professional training, or to believe that regardless of one's grades, graduation is still imminent, other activities of life seem more questionable. This is particularly evident in the quantification of some aspects of an *art* such as music.

CONCLUSION

Quantification and the many systems that man has developed over the years have provided the major basis for his environmental sophistication. Various systems of quantification combined with logical methods of analysis provide the base for experimental research. These systems are intended as vehicles toward greater understanding and should not be viewed as ends in themselves.

The student is cautioned to maintain and develop a tolerance for ambiguity. The necessity of not assuming an "either-or" attitude is again advised in relationship to quantification. The fact that man strives imperfectly toward knowledge and the development of methods to attain knowledge does not indicate that everything but the most gross subjectivity and personal biases should prevail. Many aspects of the art of music can be studied quantitatively. Perhaps, the best indication of a "closed mind" is the statement, "Well, if all that isn't *really true,* then why not forget about it." A conscientious student is capable of much more.

STUDY QUESTIONS

1. Define a "closed system." Name several in music.
2. What is meant by the statement, "Deduction is used to test observed data as a ground for induction"?
3. Devise simple experiments that illustrate each of the five Mill's Canons.
4. Give some examples of the use of numbers to give erroneous information.
5. Why should one continuously strive toward greater objectivity when quantification and mathematical systems per se do not necessarily establish truth?

CHAPTER SEVEN

the experimental process

Experimentation is just one area of research. Research in its largest definition is a process of inquiry necessitating careful and diligent investigation and studious examination. It is aimed at the discovery of interpretation of facts or practical applications of such facts. The research process is a way man has learned to *control* his inquiry. The controls one uses in the process of answering questions increase the likelihood of the answers being acceptable and functional. Scientific experimentation does not establish absolute truth, but it does move man forward in his knowledge and understanding. It is this *process* of inquiry that occupies the researcher, and the actualities that result from this controlled inquiry that provide the greatest information.

STATEMENT OF THE PROBLEM

The initial concern for the researcher is the problem to be investigated. The experimenter speculates, analyzes, and criticizes a topic deemed appropriate for research. Thus, a basic idea is advanced and analyzed to ascertain its worth and feasibility. It is criticized from known information and various points of view. Finally, it is formulated into a specific statement (hypothesis) that is testable with appropriate statistical tests.

The necessary questions pertaining to the problem are:

1. Is the logic of the problem analysis sound?
2. Is the statement of the problem in agreement with all known facts?
3. Is the problem consistent with well-known theories, and if not, how does if differ?
4. Is the problem testable and are answers attainable?

During this initial process it usually helps to talk about the project with both musicians and researchers. See if it can be explained and try to state exactly what is to be attempted. Reciprocal communication helps clarify the problem, and when it can be verbalized clearly and succinctly, it can usually be developed into a sound research design.

When the researcher begins to construct an experimental design, the basic topic is almost always altered (restricted in scope) in ways that permit it to be experimentally tested. However, a clear concept of the initial problem is still prerequisite. Even when the problem seems minutely restricted, it usually necessitates much finer delimitation before it generates specific hypotheses that can be tested. The construction of specific hypotheses represents the first refinement in the experimental process.

THE HYPOTHESIS

The word hypothesis is used in research to refer to many things. It may be the initial guess or hunch of the experimenter, it may be the tentative conclusion that is assessed after the experimental study, or it may constitute the formal statement that is to be tested. The term hypothesis (*hypo,* less than or to put under; *thesis,* position or proposition) is generally used to indicate initial supposition on a continuum from hypothesis through theory to law. A *hypothesis* is a tentative explanation; *theory* implies a greater range of evidence; *law* implies a statement of order and relation in nature that has been found to be invariable under the same conditions.

Not infrequently, the young researcher confuses a hypothesis with a law and appears determined to prove a certain position for all time. The hypothesis is the first consideration toward "truth." It is not as important for the researcher to speculate correctly as it is to investigate with extreme care. Experimentation is one method for attaining greater knowledge—it is not a game to determine "who wins." It is unlikely that the music profession will drastically change because one study "proves" a certain position. Truth is often extremely elusive. It is important that the researcher ask meaningful questions and pursue each topic carefully and *honestly*. If a tentative explanation seems unfounded, then it is important that the unfounded idea or supposition have adequate appraisal. Often, "negative results" are extremely meaningful in the structure of new experiments.

The final hypothesis should constitute the best formulation of the problem of which the experimenter is capable. While one hypothesis is often adequate, sometimes several hypotheses are necessary. The number of hypotheses depends upon the nature of the problem to be studied and upon the experimental design. It should be remembered that the rejection or substantiation of particular suppositional statements does not constitute the entire benefits of experimentation. Many times, incidental aspects of research provide the most information. Mistakes, chance factors, and research obstacles often provide new directions for the investigator. Scientific literature is replete with examples of meaningful diversions that arise from "negative aspects" of experimentation.[1]

There is a growing number of researchers who choose *not* to use formal statements to be tested (hypotheses). Instead, these experimenters prefer to investigate certain areas and let the results stand alone. They think it inadvisable to accept or reject certain sentences as being "true" or "false" and prefer to: (1) describe the area of investigation, (2) present detailed information concerning experimental procedures, and (3) present the analyzed results. For example, a researcher studying perfect pitch might initially present research literature concerning "perfect pitch." He might then state that one hundred musicians purported to have "perfect pitch" were tested on their ability to recognize fifty intervals aurally. Detailed accounts of the selection of subjects, equivalent groups, intervals, trials, evaluation of performance, and so on would be given in the design description, after which results would be presented. While statistical tests would be used to evaluate subjects' ability to recognize intervals and the differences between subjects, intervals, and so on, no attempt would be made to confirm a stated hypothesis. There would *not* be the traditional statement: "The hypothesis that subjects purported to have 'perfect pitch' recognize more selected intervals than do subjects without 'perfect pitch' is confirmed at the .05 level of significance."

Experimentation without stated hypotheses is perhaps more sophisticated and less cumbersome than traditional reporting. For the begin-

---

[1] W. I. B. Beveridge, *The Art of Scientific Investigation* (New York: Vintage Books, 1957), p. 43.

ning researcher, however, the major benefit of formulating hypotheses is the process of stating exactly what is to be investigated and tested. This process helps clarify the entire study. Of course, the *problem* of a study is always implied in the experimental design, but the initial efforts of beginning researchers are often vague at best. Therefore, all processes that help clarify the study are recommended. The hypothesis can be an initial guess, or it may represent a more general theory that is based on careful and thorough study of other research results. Regardless, the stated hypothesis needs to be specific and testable.

Hypotheses may be presented in null form (hypothesis of no difference) or, on the basis of prior research, in directional form (hypothesis of predictable difference). The researcher should realize that only well-formulated hypotheses can be tested statistically. However, the entire rationale for statistical inference makes it impossible to prove a hypothesis (Chapter Eight). When a hypothesis is said to be confirmed at the .05 level, this indicates that results could be expected to occur on the basis of *chance alone* only five times in a hundred. Truth is not established, it is approximated.

REVIEW OF LITERATURE

A necessary process in experimentation is to search the literature for specifically and generally related studies. The researcher may wish to change some aspects of the original statement of the problem after reviewing related literature. It is also strongly recommended that the researcher first review many diverse experimental studies before attempting to structure an experimental design. While it is advantageous to spend as much time in the library as possible, there are many unique topics that arise from an individual's music experiences and not from other research. These topics present a challenge because it seems that they do not have a backlog of related literature. In this case, the beginning researcher may think that an intensive review of literature would be unnecessary. However, it is most likely that: (1) a vast amount of previous research has been done in the area (although perhaps difficult for the young researcher to find), and (2) the student should demonstrate that he is aware of research in the general area even though it is not directly relevant to his topic.

Reviewing experimental literature is an exciting pursuit once the library is found. Many institutions offer courses in how to find desired information (library science, for example), but usually each student has to go through a rather difficult process in order to find exactly what he wants. Since libraries are staffed with professional personnel, it usually helps to *ask*. It is suggested that the student begin this venture when he has ample time and is relatively free from anxiety. The literature should be reviewed carefully and diligently. All possible sources should be sought (periodicals as well as books). Titles not locally available may generally be procured through inter-library loan. If the researcher is unable to locate a specific source, he should ask the librarian about other possibilities. A list of pertinent periodicals in experimental research in music and related disciplines is presented in Appendix A.

When examining the literature, it is extremely important to keep detailed accurate records of all materials for future reference and possible inclusion in the formal report. (A 4×6 card file is adequate.) Very often the researcher finds it necessary to go back to sources he has previously reviewed. It is much less difficult if these sources are immediately available. (It is somewhat like practicing your instrument—how much more practice would you get in if, when the spirit moved you, you found yourself instantaneously in the practice room with all necessary materials?) If the time it takes to keep accurate records seems exorbitant, it does not compare with the time involved in trying to find the material again—ask any advanced graduate student.

Reviewing experimental literature not only provides source material for the proposed topic, it should also help the student begin to evaluate other experiments. The student should search particularly for those experiments that appear extremely simple, for he shall soon learn that this apparent simplicity was usually earned at a tremendous price of time and effort. Design clarity often demonstrates that the researcher knew his business and was able to structure the study without undue verbiage and confusion. The student should not be deceived by thinking the process is simple. It has been said that "there are only two types of people, muddle heads and simple minds—simplicity must be earned."

THE ELEMENT OF CONTROL

The proposed hierarchy of experimental design is to: choose a topic, state the problem, construct the hypothesis, select the sample, gather the data, and analyze the results in accordance with the stated hypothesis. This sounds simple, but in fact all of these elements need to be considered simultaneously. For beginners, not only is it imperative that statistical tools (Chapter Nine) be chosen before the *collection* of the data, but also it must be remembered that when one minute aspect of the design is altered, the entire design may collapse, necessitating total revision. The student will not appreciate the many different avenues an initial topic may take until he goes through this process.

The foremost element of design is *control*. The experiment is useless unless the finished design demonstrates that all aspects of the experimental process were controlled and could not bias the experimental variable(s) other than as intended by the experimental design. The supreme concern is to know *what is influencing what*. There are countless complexities, including everything from the most obvious (precise measuring equipment) to the apparent ridiculous (color of the room in which the experiment takes place). However, many aspects previously thought ridiculous are later found to be highly significant. The researcher cannot be too careful.

The greatest single difficulty in experimental research is that the experimenter almost always has to go through many revisions before the design achieves proper scientific control. Therefore, it is preferable that the beginning researcher choose an appropriate "model experiment" for his first venture and either replicate it exactly or change just one small aspect. This is perhaps the best starting point in order for the student to *gradually* become aware of the many necessary requirements of scientific investigation. If a student chooses to go through the entire process for his initial experiment, he should be content to accept the knowledge he learns from his *mistakes* and not believe that any subsequent results should be taken seriosuly.

A FIRST EXPERIMENT

Experimentation is an exciting and rewarding experience, but like any other endeavor it has various levels of sophistication, and true competence must be earned. It is much like composition in that most musicians can write a simple tune, but a *fine* symphony takes time, artistry, and highly developed skill. Consider the case of Joe:

> Joe is a first-year graduate student and must complete a research project for a one semester course in Research Methods. Being a clarinetist, he has always wanted to know if small differences in mouthpiece sizes can be detected. This seems like an easy little experiment until someone asks how he is going to control different reed strengths, models of clarinets, and so on. He thinks about this for awhile and decides this particular experiment would be too difficult. He then decides to check trumpet mouthpieces, because it seems easier. But what brand and sizes should he test? He finally decides to test the Bach brand, because he remembers reading somewhere that they were used more often. He finally manages to obtain a "selection of Bach mouthpieces" from the local music store

(value $150.00). The mouthpiece kit contains ten different sizes.

He approaches a trumpet graduate student to talk about his project. Not only is the trumpet major seemingly unco-operative, but he lets Joe know that *he* can *always* tell the differences between mouthpieces anytime, anywhere. Right then, Joe decides he is going to run the experiment with *high school* trumpeters. He contacts the local high school and finds that they do have nine trumpet students, but they cannot be excused from school to participate. He decides to contact them individually and after fifteen telephone calls has six that will meet him in the band room two weeks from Saturday. Things are looking up, thinks Joe.

"Now, how should I test them?" he ponders. "If everyone played on each of the ten mouthpieces for three minutes, that would be one-half hour each. Oh! What happens if they get tired? (and I must remember to take a good stopwatch). I guess I will use five mouthpieces—3 $\times$ 5 = 15. I wonder if three minutes will be enough, or perhaps too much?" The next day Joe checks with another college trumpet student (not the graduate), and is told that probably one minute would be enough *if* all the trumpeters have a good warm-up. Warm-up. Joe had not thought about that. "What if they play any that morning before I can test them? I must remember to tell them not to play any before the experiment. Okay, how about the warm-up? I could give them, say, five minutes to warm up. Now, how many mouthpieces should I test?" After much deliberation, Joe decides to test just two mouthpieces, but which ones? He finally decides on the 7c and the 12c, because his trumpet friend (again not the graduate student) told him that these sizes were most often used. "Let's see now, two mouthpieces, five students—all set. Wait, how are they going to report the differences?" Joe decides to make up an answer sheet. "It could be same-different, same-different. Yeh! I will give every student the 7c, then the 12c, then the 7c, then the?? But, how much time will that take? . . . if everyone gets five trials on each mouthpiece?" Joe decides to have everyone play six times on each mouthpiece. Everything seems settled. "Now back to 'Form and Analysis' and what a tough course— it takes *so* much time. . . ."

Saturday arrives and Joe sets out with mouthpieces in hand. He arrives at the school. The heat is off and only four boys show up, one with a cornet into which the trumpet mouthpieces will not fit. The first boy looks at the number on the side of the new mouthpiece before he starts to play. "Hey, this mouthpiece is just like the one I already use." "Oh no!" Joe places a postage stamp over the number. It is all he can find. "Why didn't I think of that? Besides, I already told him *not* to look at the number." "Boy, kids are dumb these days," thinks Joe. As the boy proceeds through the test, Joe becomes even more upset because the student cannot follow Joe's directions. After two more subjects and a very harrowing morning, Joe is tremendously upset. He decides to spend the afternoon in the library.

"How do all those other people run experiments?" Joe had previously read 25 abstracts for the Research Methods class and he had also completed a critical analysis of ten original research reports. Joe decides to read one of the ten he had already reviewed and handed in. Joe thinks about that particular review assignment and what a drag it was—busy work, busy work, and besides, wasn't that the same week he had taken a mid-term in Music History? "Doesn't matter— what a morning." The first study Joe looked for was not in the library; someone had it on inter-library loan. "Fifteen minutes to find out something is not there!" Joe finally settles down with another study, and after the girl across the table left, began to concentrate. "Introduction, same old jazz —review of literature." Joe was bored. He begins to count all the sentences that start, "It would appear that . . . or, it would seem . . ." "Wow, what dull junk—third person, no personal pronouns, I wonder if Brahms could get through something like this?"

He goes to the Experimental Design section. In earnest he begins to read and suddenly he begins to see things he had overlooked before. "Subjects were randomly selected from the student rolls of ten elementary schools." "A pilot test was conducted to determine the advisability of the project." "Subjects were used as their own controls to insure construct validity." "An analysis of co-variance was used to assess performance and assign subjects to equivalent control and experimental groups." "All possible combinations of trials were randomly presented to insure control for possible order effects." "Instructions were tape-recorded and consequently, identical for all subjects." "Consistent with previous experimentation in this area, each subject was tested for only twenty minutes to control for possible fatigue." "Interims between trials were filled with recorded music to help destroy past tonal associations, which might conceivably affect results on subsequent performances." "Recordings were made in an acoustically designed studio and performances analyzed after completion of the collected data." "A detailed description of all apparatus used in the experiment is found in Appendix A." "Raw data are presented in Table IV, however, the data are quite misleading unless the statistical Table V is viewed." "While the raw data concerning subjects in Group II indicate improvement after experimental manipulation, the statistical analysis shows this to be non-significant." "The statistical analysis demonstrated individual differences to be the greatest source of variation and this could possibly account for the higher total score, but non-significance of Group II. . . ."

Joe continues to read through the report, now with greater enthusiasm. When the report refers the reader to a table, Joe actually studies the table. When he is referred to an Appendix to read instructions given to subjects, he looks in the Appendix. Joe decides to reread the entire study. He starts at the beginning and then something stops him in the middle of a page. He remembers how cold the school building was when he had tested that morning; how cold the instruments were, and how the pitch changed as the sun finally came through the windows and the room got warmer. The study he is reading concerns intonation. Joe thinks, "What about temperature? Yeh, what about temperature?" Joe hurriedly goes through the study. "Recordings were made in an acoustically designed studio," but nothing about temperature. "How about that! So this guy was a Ph.D. now and nothing about temperature." Joe looks at the beginning of the study. Sure enough, "In partial fulfillment of the degree of Doctor of Philosophy." He skips a page, "So he loves his wife and acknowledges his professors, but no temperature control and even if he did keep the temperature constant, he should have stated it."

Joe has regained his equilibrium and decides to leave. He even thinks kindly of the matronly old lady who asks to check his books. As he leaves the library, he notices how dark it has become and is only now aware of how long he has stayed, and how much he still has to do. He walks quickly toward the music building. "Yes sir, control. Control is extremely important—control all those variables that are not of experimental manipulation. No temperature, *no temperature*—if that guy can get a doctor's degree, I can, too."

CONCLUSION

The following questions are imperative in evaluating the experimental design.[2]

1. Are the experimental variables singular and not confounded with other factors or each other?
2. Are all non-manipulative variables randomized?

---

[2] Expanded coverage of these questions may be found in D. B. Van Dalen, *Understanding Education Research* (New York: McGraw-Hill Book Company, 1966).

3. Is consideration given to the possibility of the experimenter or experimental procedures signaling or otherwise biasing the results?
4. Are all precautions taken to obtain equivalence of subjects, groups, or other necessary aspects of the experiment?
5. Is the sample adequate in kind and number?
6. Are the techniques of pairing or matching valid?
7. Are there items or factors in the tests, measures or instruments, which might bias the results?
8. Was there an adequate pretesting of all aspects concerning the experiment (materials, instruments, facilities, etc.)?
9. Do the proposed samples, analysis of data, and assumptions satisfy the use of the proposed statistical procedures?
10. Can you be sure that experimental findings are the result of intended manipulations?

The "either-or" concept is never more crucial than in relationship to the experimental design. Every aspect of the design has to be considered *independently and collectively*. The experimenter is cautioned to start with an extremely simple topic and to begin to revise and limit until all of the above considerations are adequately met. Experimental design with necessary *controls* is the most important and consequently the most difficult aspect of experimental research. After the design has been structured, it represents a "recipe" that can be carried out with little difficulty. The written report should contain a specific detailed account of what actually took place in order that future researchers will be able to duplicate the study exactly without additional information. The music professions will benefit greatly from results derived from such careful experimentation.

STUDY QUESTIONS

1. What questions should be asked about the statement of the problem?
2. Select a well-known fact and trace its evolution from hypothesis through theory to law.
3. Discuss the benefits of reviewing experimental literature. What should the experimenter do if he is just completing a study and finds that it has already been done?
4. Why is *control* the most important aspect of experimental design?
5. In what ways and to what extent can you identify with Joe? Could this identification confuse, upset, or anger a person? Why?

CHAPTER EIGHT

statistical theory and musicians

Most musicians do not possess detailed knowledge of advanced statistics; in fact, many might have difficulty with simple arithmetic. These same musicians may know little about the internal combustion engine, yet they drive cars; they may not understand electronics, yet they operate phonographs; they may become confused if asked to repair a lock, yet their keys open doors. Life is far too complex to know even a small part of the world and its many attributes or man's myriad activities. However, one can usually take advantage of many products and processes if one can differentiate between them and understand *how they work*.

USES OF STATISTICS

Statistics may also be used by musicians who know very little about statistics compared to professional statisticians. This is not to advocate that the serious researcher should not learn as much as possible about statistics—and all tools of research—nor is this text intended as a substitute for formal courses in statistics. However, in any activity one must begin. Many experiments can be conducted without advanced statistical knowledge. More important, there are usually competent statisticians in institutions where research is conducted who will help the musician interested in experimental research. The musician needs to know enough to be able to effectively communicate with statisticians. It is then possible to arrive at an appropriate design with adequate evaluation of results. Computer analyses can be very useful to the experimenter because there is a large number of pre-written statistical programs that will analyze data on the basis of common statistical tests.[1] The primary concerns for the musician are: (1) to understand the general theories and vocabulary of statistics; (2) to know which statistical tools are appropriate for particular problems (design); and (3) what the results mean, that is, how to interpret the statistical findings.

Statistics are used in experimentation to: (1) describe the data, and (2) calculate relative frequency of occurrences as a ground for induction (predicting). Descriptive statistics do not present a great problem. Students are familiar with many descriptive statistics: average salary, 94th percentile, price reduction 50%, and grade point average = 3.0. Statistics used to calculate the accuracy of observations however, present a more difficult problem and necessitate some understanding of probability theory.

THEORY OF PROBABILITY

Pascal was one of the first mathematicians to explore the theory of probability in detail. Reportedly, his interest was aroused in connection with a discussion about gambling odds. He pursued the question for some time and reported many of his conclusions, published posthumously in the *Treatise on the Arithmetic Triangle* (1665).[2]

For some time afterward, the theory of probability was developed to serve as a model for games of chance. As probability theory developed, it found many uses in addition to calculating the odds for rolling dice, spinning a roulette wheel, or playing card games. It became apparent that it could also be used to serve as a model for calculation of data in science

---

[1] Assistance in the choice and application of prewritten statistical programs is generally available to students at any university that maintains a computer center.

[2] Blaise Pascal, *Treatise on the Arithmetic Triangle* (1665). See Albert Maire, Bibliographie Générale des Oeuvres de Blaise Pascal, Paris: L. Giraud Badin, 1925.

and empirical experimentation.[3] A common characteristic of the gambler and scientist is that neither knows precisely what each individual outcome will be. Each must calculate in relation to the long run. *Given that certain things are true,* deductions may be made concerning what should be true *in the long run.* Every student who is faced with a decision goes through a similar process, although perhaps not as stringently. Underlying all statistical calculations is one basic tautology. *Events may be expected to move in the direction in which it is most probable they will move.* Thus, if the initial premise is true, or assumed to be true, it can be tested using the theory of probability for verification and possible prediction.

For example, most of us assume that the probability for tossing a coin either heads or tails is .50. Suppose that one was given a coin and asked to devise an experiment to see if the coin was fair, that is, if the probability of tossing heads is indeed .50. (The student is asked to take a coin and conduct this experiment.) Suppose that we decide to toss the coin ten times, keeping an accurate account of the occurrences of heads. Do it. If the student did this, he should not be surprised if the number of heads was less or more than five. Now suppose the coin is tossed ten more times and the total number of heads from the first ten tosses combined with that from the second ten tosses. Still the student should not be surprised if the total number of heads was more or less than ten. This process could be continued indefinitely. At what point (number of samplings) could one be reasonably sure that the coin was indeed fair? Put another way, if your life depended upon your correct assessment of the fairness of *your* coin, how many trials would you prefer to make before declaring that your coin is fair or biased? Think about it. If the student actually conducted this simple experiment and contemplated correct assessment in terms of his own life, he should begin to realize some of the attributes of the theory of probability and the number of trials required for accurate judgment. In addition, the uncertainty of absolute assessment, regardless of how many tosses, should be apparent. If the coin is indeed fair (proportion of heads = .50), then one can expect the observed proportion to approach .50 in the long run. A statement of probability tells us what to *expect* about the relative frequency of an event, given that enough sample observations are made at random. Since similar observations have previously been made many times regarding coins, we know (or at least strongly suspect) that the probability that our coin will turn up heads = .50. Thus, we can make the statement

---

[3] For an excellent historical overview of the beginnings of probability theory, see the classical work by I. Todhunter, *A History of the Mathematical Theory of Probability* (Cambridge: MacMillian, 1865).

of probability "that for any given toss of the coin, the probability of heads is .50." The thoughtful student may realize that if this is the case *for each trial,* then the possibility exists that the coin may come up heads every time. While this is possible, it is tremendously unlikely. One need only engage in a little gambling to fully realize this concept.[4] There would be no need for probability theory if *all* observations could be assessed. It is the necessity for ipso facto decisions which requires some basis for calculation. Without probability theory, generalization would be without method, and scientific experimentation would have little meaning.

Statistical theory and the laws of probability have become very important in modern life. Constantly, one hears the phrases, "in all probability," "the law of averages," or "relatively constant." These are statistical concepts concerning the laws of chance. Insurance companies represent an excellent example. If it were not for calculations based on the laws of probability, these companies could not exist. While it is not possible to predict the exact time any one person, age twenty, will die, an actuary is able to predict quite accurately how many twenty-year-olds will die this year, next year, and so on. Another example is the beginning of banking, when the old safe owner found that he could loan out another's money because not all of his depositors came to take their money out at the same time. Provisions have subsequently been made to insure depositors' money because of early speculation that sometimes proved excessive. Rates for this insurance (FDIC) are again based on the number of faulty speculations and thus the laws of probability. It is difficult to imagine many aspects of modern life that do not use and benefit from the application of this theory.

REQUIREMENTS FOR STATISTICAL DESCRIPTIONS

It should be apparent from foregoing discussions (Chapter Six) that the first requirement for statistical analysis is a means whereby data can be quantitatively assessed. *Measurement* involves assignment of numbers to observable phenomena. The process, as previously indicated, represents a tenuous transfer; however, it is the best means available, and careful procedures will assure greater "meaning" of the results. It is important not to ascribe numbers to aspects of data that are indeed

---

4 Gambling houses capitalize on the independence of trials (if the houses are fair). For example, if one were to bet on red continuously on a roulette wheel, he would "in the long run" lose some of his money. Remember that there are "green" spaces. These are certainly not included for reasons of aesthetic interior decor.

different and then treat them as if they were similar. Each particular event of observation within an experiment should represent a point in a well-defined area of·investigation. Thus, if one is measuring intonation, some objective numerical terminology is necessary that *does not include many different aspects simultaneously.* A negative example would be a rating scale that included only one numerical classification combining flatness, sharpness, type of instrument, grade level, I.Q., years of study, and so on. Discrimination and separate differentiation of categories with appropriate numerical description are imperative.

There are four general types of measurement scales used in experimentation: (1) nominal, (2) ordinal, (3) interval, and (4) ratio. The *nominal,* or "naming," scale is used solely for classification, for example, flat–sharp, good–bad, large, improvement. The only relation involved in the nominal scale is of equality or differences, and members must be identifiable by the property being scaled. For example, a large chorus is easily classified nominally into soprano, alto, tenor, or bass. The nominal scale represents the weakest basis for assessment, and only non-parametric statistics (discussed later) are appropriate for these kinds of data.

The *ordinal* scale not only allows comparisons of equality and differences but also permits the rank ordering of members of a group or events. Statements such as less than ($<$) or greater than ($>$) can also be designated, but the *number of times* one member is greater than or less than another or the *relative differences* between observations cannot be assessed. The assignment of orchestral parts within a section on the basis of assessed proficiency (auditions) is an excellent example of ordinal scaling by the conductor. Again, only non-parametric statistics are appropriate.

An *interval* scale permits measurement of equality and differences of *intervals* and also greater-than and less-than measurements. This scale permits the assessment of intervalic comparisons. The chromatic scale on the equal-tempered piano represents interval scaling at its best, that is, C$\sharp$ is to D as D is to D$\sharp$, and so on. An interval scale does not need an absolute zero point; however, the distances between points on the scale are of known size (common examples are the metronome, thermometer, and calendar). An interval scale is perhaps the strongest scale that can be used for most experimental research in music. More powerful methods of statistical analysis, that is, parametric statistics, are possible when interval scaling can be achieved.

The *ratio* scale has all of the above characteristics but also has an absolute zero point. This allows values to be doubled, tripled, etc. Some apparatus for measuring pitch and duration (for example, Stroboconn, electric clock) represent possibilities for ratio scaling, for example, stroboscopic analysis of pitch in plus or minus cent deviations and timings of durational rhythmic patterns. The ratio scale meets all the requirements for parametric statistical analysis and is to be preferred whenever possible.

After any of the above measurements have been made, often there needs to be some orderly arrangement of the observations so that pertinent facts may be *described*. Some assessment needs to be made concerning the extent to which these observations differ in magnitude and how they are distributed in value. One process for accomplishing this is called a *frequency distribution*. This consists of recording all the possible scores and then counting the number (frequency) of scores having each particular score value. When this is accomplished, the experimenter can then describe in what interval class (classes) most of the scores are concentrated and, also, where there is a sparsity of scores.

CENTRAL TENDENCY

A frequency distribution is a summary of data, but for many purposes it is necessary to summarize still further. Two characteristics of an observed distribution are its measures of *central tendency* and *variability*. If a student were instructed to choose one score from a group of many scores to best describe an entire distribution, an "average" score would probably be chosen. However, there are at least three different "averages" that could be specified: (1) the most frequent or commonly attained score—*mode,* (2) the point exactly midway between the top and bottom scores of the distribution—*median,* or (3) the familiar arithmetic average of the distribution—*mean.* If the mean, mode, and median are the same, then the distribution of scores is symmetrical. A common representation is the familar bell-shaped curve.

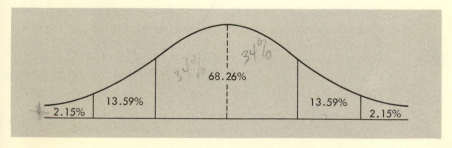

"NORMAL" DISTRIBUTION

In any kind of measurement regardless of how careful observers try to be, small differences will occur. Thus, if 1000 musicians were given stopwatches and instructed to measure the precise time it takes for an individual to perform a certain rhythmic pattern, there would be many slightly different timings. If these timings (observations) were charted, it is extremely likely that the graph constructed from the distribution of these measurements would constitute a *normal curve*. This amazing characteristic of observations falling into a normal distribution can be demonstrated in such natural phenomena as sizes of feet, colors of hair, and heights of trees, and in the chance distribution of factors upon which the theories of probability rest.[5] For example, consider the probability of tossing different numbers of heads for ten coins, much like your earlier experiment. However, instead of tossing one coin ten times, think of tossing ten coins one time each. What would be the probability of obtaining 0, 1, 2, 3, . . . , 10 heads?

No. of Heads	Probability
10	1/1,024
9	10/1,024
8	45/1,024
7	120/1,024
6	210/1,024
5	252/1,024
4	210/1,024
3	120/1,024
2	45/1,024
1	10/1,024
0	1/1,024

It is easily observed that the above probabilities (binomial distribution) are approximated by the normal curve. The normal curve is regarded as a mathematical ideal and comparisons between samples of observation and this mathematical ideal provide the basis for important inferences.

Any index of central tendency, whether it be the mean, mode, or median, summarizes only one aspect of a distribution. Most experimental distributions have at least one other attribute called *spread* or *dispersion*. This is the tendency for observations to depart or deviate from central tendency. Descriptive statistics of this type are called measures of *variability*.

---

[5] A discussion of the principles upon which these ideas rest can be obtained through study of any good elementary textbook. Selected references for students of music are included in Appendix B.

Two measures of variability generally used in research are the *standard deviation* and the *variance*. The standard deviation is simply the square root of the variance. To compute the variance, we: (1) subtract each score from the mean (the result is called a deviation), (2) square each deviation, (3) add the squared deviations, and (4) divide by the number of scores minus 1. To compute the standard deviation, we simply extract the square root of the variance. Also, by subtracting the mean from an individual score and dividing by the standard deviation, the individual score is transformed to a *standard score* (z score). The use of standard scores allows a description of a subject's position in a given distribution with respect to both mean and variability, and makes direct comparisons with other distributions possible. Through the use of tables, the z scores can be converted to *percentile ranks*.[6]

The mean, standard deviation, and standardized scores are useful devices for summarizing data. However, the essence of these simple devices is that they provide fundamental cornerstones for inferential statistics.

SAMPLING AND RANDOMNESS

Since one of the foremost requirements for all statistical inference is the necessity of proper sampling techniques, the concepts of sampling and randomness need to be understood. The process of gathering data is called *sampling*. The results themselves are called observations, and a collection of observations is called a *sample* (a collection of observed sample events).

The term *random* is another extremely important term, denoting several important statistical procedures. The basic concept of randomness is simple. It signifies that each element of the sample has an equal and independent probability of being the sample selected; that is, *there is a lack of fixed pattern or order*. Before a die is thrown, the six possibilities are random because there is not a fixed order or pattern for each throw (that is, each throw represents a single miniature experiment). Each of the six numbers has an equal probability of coming up. (The student is reminded that it was the problem of calculating the odds for certain gambling possibilities that initiated the study of statistical inference.) The importance of this "randomness" permeates experimental research. If various possibilities of events are to remain free from systematic bias, then randomness must be assured. No one would desire to

---

[6] Problems of this type, in addition to many others, can be solved with elementay knowledge and a source including various conversion tables. See Appendix B.

walk into a gambling situation where someone held "loaded dice." In a dice game, the possibilities (twelve numbers) need to be known and the participant must be assured that each possible number has an equal opportunity of coming up, that is, of being selected. Such is the case with statistics. After the experiment is completed, the researcher wants to be certain that the results were free from any systematic bias; that differences resulting from experimental manipulation (treatments) were caused by the manipulation, and did not result from uncontrolled factors. The essence of *experimental control* is that (1) aspects of the experiment that should be random are indeed randomly determined (sampling techniques), and (2) aspects not free to vary are controlled so they do not bias the results (experimental methodology). When researchers speak of rejecting experiments "that are not controlled," they are referring to inadequacies concerning sampling or methodology.

Randomness is usually thought of in reference to selecting samples, but it can also refer to selecting trials, mixing up orders of trials and presentations, assigning subjects to various treatment groups, and any other procedure of experimentation that necessitates controlling for undesired bias. For example, a researcher may take great care in selecting subjects at random but then proceed to give trials (for example, pitches) that have a fixed order that could bias the experiment (order effect). In this case, how does one know that the *order of presentation* (sequential pitches) is not influencing the results; that any differences in one trial are not caused by another trial or by the accumulation of successive presentations? This particular aspect of testing order effects could represent a separate experiment in itself, where the researcher presents certain trials in a fixed order to test if the *order* makes any difference.

The primary consideration in the process of randomness is to insure that all possibilities have an equal chance of being selected. If the experimenter selects every third student from a chosen population, or presents every second rhythmic variation from a group of selected rhythms, this would not represent randomness, because a fixed pattern would be evident. Random selection or random arrangement can be made by using tables of random numbers, by drawing numbers from a hat, by mixing up all possibilities and selecting by chance, or upon any other basis that insures equal possibility of selection or arrangement.

Sampling and randomness are extremely important. It should also be noted that there is no way to "cheat" the laws of probability regarding sampling and methodology. If the manipulation of experimental variables produces a statistically-significant variation different from what would be expected by chance alone, this variation will be evident. If the effect of experimental manipulation is not greater than that expected by chance only, then there will be no statistically-significant differences. It should be remembered that statistical tools constitute a "double-edged sword." If "expected results" are forthcoming in an experiment where the design is suspect because of uncontrolled variables, then "results" are discounted. If the structure of the design is inadequate to test desired information because principles of random selection are ignored and *cancel a real variation,* the experiment still fails because it does not demonstrate results that *actually may exist.* Even predictions of professional statisticians have been subsequently proven wrong many times. This happens not because the statistical tools are inadequate, but because methods of sampling were biased and not truly representative of what later proved to be the actual case; that is, the real population or uncontrolled variables were left free to vary. The experimenter is advised to design carefully. The more subtle the variables being investigated, the more precise the design needs to be.

Concerning sampling, the question has been asked many times—*how large does the sample need to be?* The answer is that the sample should be as large as necessary to accord with the importance of the question under investigation. Remember your coin-tossing experiment. How large would you want the sample (number of tosses) to be if your life depended on it? In this instance, the larger the sample the better. Obviously, the larger the sample, the greater is the possibility of ascertaining the actual case. However, sample size alone should not be confused with the importance of the study. Many results that are statistically significant because they are based on a large sample are neither musically nor actually important. The question "if your life depended on it" is far-fetched for many instances, yet daily life evidences certain risks. While many do not choose to play "Russian Roulette," we still drive automobiles, hunt, smoke, and engage in many activities if we feel the odds are in our favor. Perhaps we do not even think about it. Almost all man's activities have been calculated statistically, because *adequate sampling techniques* have made it possible. The beginning researcher should examine many studies in various disciplines to see what others consider an adequate sample, and determine whether the area warrants further investigation. If a significant result is obtained with a sample of 30, it can be generally assumed that the area is worthy of more extensive investigation. The student will find that time and physical circumstances usually help to determine the size of the sample. He should try to make the sample as large as is feasible, depending on his value judgments to determine the importance of the area. A large sample might produce significant results with very small differences that would not be worthwhile for anyone to know. Statistical significance is a tool for making judgments and is not the ultimate court of psychological, musical, or practical importance. If slight deviations in muscle tension are studied in 2000 violin players by means of an EMG, and we find significantly more tension in those who play poorly, but no teacher is able to detect the difference, then we have a statistically-significant result of no practical application. However, any study may lead to cumulative knowledge that might eventually produce practical application. The larger the sample, the greater is the probability that it represents the actual or theoretical population—*if random selection is insured.*[7]

CONCLUSION

Statistical methods and measurements cannot be separated. They do *not* constitute an "either-or"; both need to be considered simultaneously. Statistics are useless without measurements, and without statistics experimental investigation would not provide much useful information. Statistical evaluations provide the researcher with many advantages.

1. They permit a more exact description.
2. They necessitate clear thinking and exactness in experimental design.
3. They enable summarization of results in more interpretable forms.
4. They provide a method whereby inferences can be made to predict other eventualities.[8]

STUDY QUESTIONS

1. How are statistics used in experimental research?
2. Explain the theory of probability. What common uses does this theory have?
3. Name the four general types of measurement scales and give examples of each.
4. What is meant by central tendency? To what does it apply?
5. Define sampling and randomness. How do they interrelate? How are they different? What is meant by "systematic bias?"

[7] This section represents an extremely condensed overview for the neophyte music researcher. Entire volumes have been written pertaining to only a few of the many concepts advanced in these few pages (e.g., fixed-random variables, areas of rejection under Ho, Type I & II errors, etc.). The instructor may wish to pursue some of these concepts in greater detail; the student is referred to Appendix B.

[8] Adapted from J. P. Guilford, *Fundamental Statistics in Psychology and Education* (New York: McGraw-Hill, 1965), pp. 3–4.

CHAPTER NINE

elementary statistical tests

This chapter deals with some common statistical tests deemed appropriate for research designs in music. The statistical test should be chosen before the experiment is conducted. Again, it should be stated that this is imperative for the beginning researcher. However, the musician should not become distressed. Statistics should not represent a mystical or frightening void for the beginner. The process of choosing the appropriate statistical test is not a problem of "working out an experiment and then worrying about finding something to evaluate it." Statistical tests are structured to *coincide* with the experimental design. These tests have been developd with the express purpose of evaluating data, and most experimental designs are very similar in all fields of scientific investigation. Areas of experimental interest, populations, and observations under investigation may be quite different, but the basic experimental designs are really quite simple and similar.

PARAMETRIC AND NON-PARAMETRIC STATISTICS

Statistical tests are separated into two distinct groups, *parametric* and *non-parametric*. A parameter is a quantity that describes a population. A population is defined as that particular set of observations, however measured, from which samples of observations may be drawn. A population of observations is determined by the experimenter. He may be interested in observations of a group of people, a colony of mice, a selection of instruments, brands of mouthpieces, a range of pitches, differential rhythmic patterns, or any other conceivable population of defined experimental interest. If a mean were computed for the different sizes of mouthpieces representing a defined population (all trumpet mouthpieces), this mean could be a parameter. Parametric tests do not require the experimenter to know all of the actual population values. If all values were known, there would be no reason for the tests. Statistical manipulations make it possible to make inferences about the parameters of the population from which the samples were drawn, hence the term, parametric tests.

There are three assumptions upon which parametric tests are based:

1. That samples are drawn from a population with a known distribution. (Normal distributions are generally assumed.)
2. That variances of all samples are homogeneous.
3. That variables to be measured achieve *interval* measurement (cf., p. 70).

All of the above, especially the third assumption, are necessary for parametric tests. Parametric statistical tests require interval scale measurement, whereas non-parametric tests do not specify all of these conditions. A ratio scale is preferred to an interval scale if the data qualify. For example, intonation investigations where performances are measured on the chromatic stroboscope (Stroboconn) represent ratio measurement. Parametric tests are more *powerful;* that is, they generally yield the same results with smaller samples, and should be used when interval measurements are achieved. Among the most common parametric tests for testing differences in means are the various *t* tests, and analyses of variance.

The primary characteristic of *non-parametric* tests is that they do not require interval measurement and can deal with nominal and ordinal (ranking) measurements. The only assumption necessitated by these tests is that observations are independent. Non-parametric tests are used when interval measurement cannot be achieved or when ordinal measurement is preferred (for example, the use of chi square in questionnaire analysis).

The qualifications and specific requirements of the data to be analyzed are much more important than the choice concerning parametric or non-parametric tests. Statistical analysis is not a "game" where one chooses any test which might demonstrate the greatest "results." Extreme care should be taken to seek professional advice *before* the data are collected to assure the experimenter that adequate precautions have been taken in the structure of the design in the collection of data and in the employment of appropriate statistical tests that best assess the significance of the variables being investigated. The usual procedure is to state the null hypothesis and (1) select a significance level that minimizes the likelihood of rejecting this null hypothesis if it is indeed true (Type I error), and (2) select a sample size (N) that minimizes the likelihood of accepting this null hypothesis when it is indeed false (Type II error). There is a direct relationship between these two errors. However, intervalic measurement, as opposed to ranking, generally decreases the probability of making the Type I error. Also, as N increases, the probability of making the Type II error generally decreases.

CORRELATIONS

In a controlled experiment, samples are generally manipulated in some manner, and the effect of the manipulation is assessed (for example, effects of programmed instruction in sight singing). Often, the researcher does not or cannot use certain techniques because of ethical considerations (for example, will a tone stimulus of 200 db cause deafness?). A researcher may choose to study the relationship between two different sets of observations. In this case, correlations are made between two sets of scores or variables (for example, deafness and factory noise). The degree of correspondence between two sets of scores is expressed as a *correlation coefficient* (r) whose obtained value is expressed from +1.00 to −1.00. A value of +1.00 indicates a *perfect positive* correlation, a value of zero indicates no correlation and a value of −1.00 indicates a *perfect inverse* relationship. A high coefficient or, in fact, any relationship *does not imply causality*. Although, if it is known that a high r exists between two variables, it is possible to predict one of these variables by knowing the other. At what level a correlation should be taken seriously poses a difficult question. It is generally accepted that anything over .70 represents a high correlation; however, interpretation depends upon the variables and the sample size, and is also based upon the purpose for which the r was calculated. (A correlation of .70 should never be confused with 70 percent or the 70th percentile. These statistics represent three separate descriptions.)

The *Spearman correlation coefficient* and *Kendall's Tau* are nonparametric techniques that can be used to calculate correlations when measurements are ordered according to rank. *Pearson's product-moment* correlation is another technique generally computed on the basis of actual scores.

ONE-SAMPLE METHOD

The one-sample study consists of determining whether the selected observations came from a specified population, either theoretical or known. After the observations have been quantified, the data are compared to a theoretical distribution to see how "good it fits" (*goodness-of-fit tests:* χ^2, *binomial test, Kolmogorov-Smirnov one-sample test*). If interval measurement has been achieved, a *t* test (parametric) can be used to determine whether the mean of the sample is the same or different from the mean of the theoretical population distribution. If nominal measurements are achieved, then the chi square (χ^2) one-sample test or binomial test should be used. The *Kolmogorov-Smirnov one-sample test* is used for ranked data. If interval measurements are achieved, the *t* test is preferred.

The rationale for the goodness-of-fit tests as *tests of significance* is based on the assumption that after samples have been drawn at random from a specified population, the error in sampling can be assessed in relationship to the theoretical distribution so that inferences can be made about the sample. The process of goodness-of-fit testing represents: (1) assuming a known or theoretical distribution for a particular population, (2) extracting samples from the larger population, and (3) checking these observations against a theoretical distribution on the basis of sampling error. The experimenter may be concerned with whether or not observations are the *same* as the theoretical distribution, whether or not observations are *significantly different* from results obtained on the basis of chance alone, or other questions that will determine the statement of the hypothesis.

The chi square enjoys great popularity in analyzing questionnaire results where the investigator wishes to know if results deviate significantly from an expected frequency. He might hypothesize that all responses will fall evenly over the possible answers, and this becomes the *expected frequency*. The *observed frequency* for each answer is compared to each expected frequency, and significance determined. The χ^2 may also be used to assess the significance of before and after treatment designs when responses obtained prior to treatment are considered to be the expected frequencies, responses after treatment, the observed frequencies.

TWO-SAMPLE METHOD

When samples from a defined population are assigned to two independent groups or to two equivalent (matched) groups, the experimenter has a control sample for comparison with the experimental sample. This two-sample design is generally superior to the one-sample method because of extra control and should be used if possible. The one-sample method usually makes comparisons based on a non-existent "theoretical control group." In the two-sample method, a control group actually exists; therefore, the question is asked, is there a difference between the two samples *after* treatment? That is, do they now come from the same or different populations? Appropriate statistical tests for the two-sample independent method include the *t* test for independent samples (parametric), the *Mann-Whitney U test* (ordinal) and the chi square (χ^2) for independent samples (nominal).

When the two samples can be matched according to some appropriate criterion, the design is called an *Equivalent Sample Method*. Matching may be achieved on the basis of prior information or current tests (for example, I.Q., G. P. A., music tests, sex, socio-economic scales, age, music experience), or a pre-test may be constructed. *Unless the matching procedure is specifically appropriate to the experiment, it is better to assign subjects randomly to the control and experimental treatments.* A frequent mistake in educational research is to match subjects on commonly-used tests that may have nothing to do with the experiment except to interfere with equality of groups. For example, using I.Q. scores to assign sixty musicians to either a sight singing manipulation or to a control group might bias the experimental results without serving as a matching device. A relevant pre-test that indeed serves to match subjects and thereby insures equality of groups may be specially-constructed. Important benefits can be derived from the pre-test–post-test designs: (1) subjects can be used as their own controls; that is, performance of each subject can be compared for before and after treatment effects; (2) subjects can be randomly assigned to control and experimental groups on the basis of pre-test scores; and (3) "matched" subjects more narrowly define the population and represent a more monolithic group.

Appropriate statistical tests for two equivalent matched samples are the *t test* (interval), the *sign test* (nominal), *The McNemar test for the significance of changes* (nominal), and the *Wilcoxon matched pairs signed-rank test* (ordinal).

MULTIPLE-SAMPLE METHOD

The *multiple-sample method* designs are considered to represent sophisticated methods of experimental research. As with the two-sample methods, samples are either equivalent or independent.

If the experienced investigator is able to obtain the use of a pre-written statistical computer program or the services of a professional statistician, he should strongly consider one of the more sophisticated designs (that is, a design with a control group[s]). Unless the nature of the topic of experimental interest is prohibitive, the researcher should try to achieve all of the aforementioned qualifications of parametric statistics and advanced design. It is often more difficult to design an experiment that is vague, inadequate, and lacking in control than to strive for quality research. If evaluation equipment is available to achieve interval measurement, it should be used (stroboscope, oscilloscope, standard time, and so on). If interval or ratio measurement can be attained, the experimenter should not settle for anything less. If it is appropriate to the study that subjects be matched, if pre-test and post-test measures are constructed, and/or if possible rotation of groups is accomplished, the researcher should not be content to do inadequate research. If the researcher plans to spend a great amount of time on the research project, it would appear wise to construct the best design possible.

Rotation of experimental variables (subjects, groups, trials, stimuli, and so on) is a process of changing or alternating situations. The experimenter may also choose to alternate samples in a multiple sample study to assess observed results when different samples are exposed to treatment, or he may desire to assess the relative effect(s) of a variable change (for example, intensity, rate, duration, or order). Various *factorial* designs abound to (1) provide the researcher with methods that evaluate the presentation of several variables and their interactions simultaneously, and to (2) statistically *evaluate* the singular and interactive effects of these many variables (*analyses of variance tests*).

A word of caution should be given the beginning researcher. When variables are presented in different combinations or when the researcher desires to control or randomize many variables, he must consider the magnitude of vast possibilities. For example, the possible combinations of two events are expressed $2 \times 1 = 2$. The possibilities of three are expressed $3 \times 2 \times 1 = 6$, of four $4 \times 3 \times 2 \times 1 = 24$, of five $5 \times 4 \times 3 \times 2 \times 1 = 120$, and so on. Not only does this magnitude apply to structuring the experimental events (trials, rotations, and so on), it also necessitates appropriate statistical tests (for example, *factorial analysis of variance*) and increased complexity of interpretation. It is the problem of evaluating designs of this magnitude that generally *requires* the use of a computer. It should be remembered that the pre-written computer programs ("canned programs") may be used for almost all of the common statistical tests, regardless of the magnitude of the data.

Statistical tests for two or more *independent samples* include the parametric *analysis of variance*, the non-parametric *Kroskal-Wallis one-way analysis of variance by ranks*, and the *chi square* (χ^2) *test for more than two independent groups.* Appropriate statistical tests for more than two equivalent samples include the various parametric *analyses of variance and co-variance.* The non-parametrics include the *Cochran Q test* and the *Friedman two-way analysis of variance by ranks.*

The parametric *analyses of variance* are perhaps the most widely used in all of experimental research in the behavioral sciences. These tests are sometimes referred to as *F* tests and provide information to evaluate significance levels from an *F* table. The analysis of variance is a technique for dividing the variation observed in experimental data into different parts, each assignable to a known source, cause, factor, or interaction. The relative magnitude of variation resulting from different sources can be assessed and the hypotheses of experimental interest either accepted or rejected. (See Edwards for discussion of one- and two-tail tests.) In its simplest form, the analysis is used to test the significance of the differences between sample means. If data qualify, the one-way or two-way analysis is recommended. The three-way, four-way, or more complex analyses of variance are extremely useful when many separate observations of different pitches or rhythms need to be analyzed, thus necessitating the calculation of many interactions. Expanded coverage of principles, tests, and design problems is available to the more sophisticated researcher but necessitates advanced work in statistics and experimental design. Following is a chart of selected research designs and statistical tests.[1]

CONCLUSION

Experiments may generally be classified in one of three groups: (1) the One-Sample Method, where a sample is drawn from a population and compared, assessing the chance factors of sampling (null hypothesis) to the larger sample from which it was drawn or by the preferred pre-test–post-test design; (2) the Two-Sample Method, where samples are drawn, treated differently, and the differences between samples compared (independent samples), or matched and compared to each other (equivalent samples); and (3) the Multiple-Sample Method (independent or equivalent), which may represent three-way, four-way, or other factorial comparisions. Rotation of samples may be used in any of the above categories. Rotation designs sometimes provide greater control and greater informa-

---

[1] A more comprehensive discussion of experimental design and statistical tests will be found in two excellent sources: *Experimental and Quasi-Experimental Designs for Research,* Donald T. Campbell and Julian C. Stanley (Chicago: Rand McNally & Co., 1963) and *Nonparametric Statistics, Sidney Siegel* (New York: McGraw-Hill Book Company, 1956).

Hypothesis of No Difference (two-tail)

Hypothesis of Predictable Difference (one-tail)
Area of rejection when p = .05

One-Sample

Post-test only	Pre-test Post-test
XO	X_1X_2O O_1XO_2

Classification or ranking	Subjects as own control
$O_1O_2O_3O_4O_5$ etc.	$O_1XO_2XO_3$

Two-Sample

Equivalent

Post-test only	Pre-test Post-test
M $\begin{array}{l}XO\\O\end{array}$	M $\begin{array}{l}O_1XO_2\\O_1\ \ O_2\end{array}$
M $\begin{array}{l}X_1O\\X_2O\end{array}$	O_1M $\begin{array}{l}XO_2\\O_2\end{array}$

Independent

Post-test only	Pre-test Post-test
$\begin{array}{l}XO\\O\end{array}$	$\begin{array}{l}O_1XO_2\\O_1\ \ O_2\end{array}$
$\begin{array}{l}X_1O\\X_2O\end{array}$	O_1 $\begin{array}{l}XO_2\\O_2\end{array}$

Multiple-Sample

Equivalent

Post-test only	Pre-test Post-test	Temporal
M $\begin{array}{l}XO\\XO\\O\end{array}$	$\begin{array}{l}MO_1XO_2\\MO_1\ \ O_2\\M\ \ XO_1\\M\ \ O_1\end{array}$	$\begin{array}{l}MO_1X_1O_2X_2O_3X_3O_4\\MO_1\ \ O_2X_2O_3X_3O_4\\MO_1\ \ O_2\ \ O_3X_3O_4\\MO_1\ \ O_2\ \ O_3\ \ O_4\end{array}$

Matching by Counterbalance:
$\begin{array}{l}X_1OX_2OX_3OX_4O\\X_3OX_1OX_4OX_2O\\X_4OX_3OX_2OX_1O\\X_4OX_3OX_2OX_1O\end{array}$

Independent

Pre-test Post-test	Counterbalance	Temporal
$\begin{array}{l}O_1XO_2\\O_1X_2O_2\\O_1\ \ O_2\end{array}$	$\begin{array}{l}X_1OX_2OX_3OX_4O\\X_2OX_4OX_1OX_3O\\X_3OX_1OX_4OX_2O\\X_4OX_3OX_2OX_1O\end{array}$	$\begin{array}{l}O_1X\ O_2O_3O_4O_5\\O_1O_2X\ O_3O_4O_5\\O_1O_2O_3X\ O_4O_5\\O_1O_2O_3O_4X\ O_5\\O_1O_2O_3O_4\ \ O_5\end{array}$

NOMINAL MEASUREMENT

χ^2 One-Sample Test. Goodness of fit for testing expected vs. observed frequencies (e.g., preferences among defined categories on questionnaire, performance rating scale, etc.). **Binomial Test.** Goodness of fit for testing two discrete categories (e.g., flat-sharp, loud-soft, correct-incorrect).

McNemar Test for Significance of Changes. Used when the two categories are not related in measurement levels i.e., when one or both categories achieve only nominal level (e.g., comparing musical judgments good-bad with rank order judgments). Excellent when subject acts as own control.

Fisher Exact Probability Test. Used with small N to test differences between samples on basis of central tendency in a 2×2 table. **χ^2 Test for Independent Samples.** Used to test differences between samples on basis of *any* discrete differences between the two populations.

Cochran Q Test. Used to test whether three or more matched sets differ significantly among themselves on the basis of dichotomous data (e.g., yes-no, flat-sharp, correct-incorrect). Matching may be between different subjects or on different observations for each subject.

χ^2 Test for Multiple Independent Samples. Used to test significant differences among samples.

ORDINAL MEASUREMENT	*Kolmogorov-Smirnov One-Sample Test.* Goodness of fit for testing ranked data (e.g., pre- vs. post-test measures, questionnaire, performance rating scale). Preferred to χ^2 if sample is small.	*Wilcoxon Matched Pairs.* Used when measurements achieve ordinal level both between and within pairs. *Sign test.* Used when ordinal measurements achieved only within pairs.	*Mann-Whitney U.* Used to test differences in samples on basis of central tendency. Most powerful alternate to the parametric t test. *Kolmogorov-Smirnov Two-Sample Test.* Used to test significance between samples on basis of *any* differences between populations (two-tail) or central tendency (one-tail).	*Friedman Two-Way Analysis of Variance.* Used to test whether three or more matched sets differ significantly among themselves on basis of mean ranks for each set.	*Kruskal-Wallis One-Way Analysis of Variance.* Used to test significant differences among samples on basis of ranks. This test is always preferred to χ^2 if data qualify.
INTERVAL OR RATIO MEASUREMENT	*t Test.* Used to test significance between the sample mean and theoretical distribution or pre- and post-test differences.	*t Test.* Used to test significance between related sample means or means of different scores. *Walsh Test.* Used to test significance between samples of ranked differences when N is less than 15.	*t Test.* Used to test significance between independent sample means. *Randomization Test for Two Independent Samples.* Used to test significance between independent sample means. Should be used with small N.	*Analysis of Variance.* Used to test whether three or more matched samples differ significantly among themselves on basis of variance between sample means.	*Analysis of Variance.* Used to test whether three or more independent samples differ significantly on basis of variance between sample means.

X = Experimental Variable (treatments)

O = Observation (measurements)

M = Matching on basis of known attributes or pre-test by pairs of subjects, groups, or by using each subject as own control

tion, although it should be stated that these designs are often more difficult to structure and evaluate.

Comparisons are based on the laws of probability, as are, in fact, all statistical tests. The student may imagine that in the simplest experiment (like the one conducted in Chapter Eight concerning the fairness of your coin) only one theoretical distribution is being employed (binomial). As each new dimension is added in an experiment, interpretation becomes more complex. The entire rationale for statistical comparisons concerns the laws of probability based upon various distributions (normal, x^2, t, and so on). Statistical tests should be chosen with primary regard to the qualification requirements of the data in relationship to the entire experimental design.

STUDY QUESTIONS

1. List the differences between the requirements and uses of parametric and nonparametric tests.
2. Discuss the advisability of using a two-sample method as opposed to using a one-sample method.
3. In what types of investigations would correlation techniques be advisable? What is meant by a perfect positive correlation; perfect inverse relationship?
4. What is the null hypothesis? What is the rationale for rejecting it? What is meant by a one-tail test as opposed to a two-tailed test?
5. Discuss the three groups of experimental classifications. How do these differ? How do they compare to the Mill's Canons?

CHAPTER TEN

completion of an experiment

The student has been introduced to experimental control, decisions involving the choices of common statistical tests, and the fact that all aspects of experimental procedures need to be considered before structuring the design. The student should now consider instrumentation of the experiment. As instrumentation is developed, the design will gradually be formulated, and statistical tests can be chosen with regard to numerical classifications.

INSTRUMENTATION

Instrumentation involves tests, appraisal instruments, evaluating apparatus, or any implements necessary to measure observed data. The basic question of instrumentation is how responses are to be measured. For example, a study of intonational performance accuracy may be measured by the chromatic stroboscope and data recorded in plus and minus cent deviations from equal temperament. A rhythmic study may be assessed in time deviations from an established standard as measured by an electric metronome or standard timer. A study of the influence of music on behavior (affective responses to music) may be measured by written responses on a numerical scale constructed by the investigator, and so on. Some problems arise concerning elaborate measuring devices, but many simple experiments can be conducted with the use of a tape recorder, metronome, Stroboconn, record player, or other available apparatus (Descriptions of common measuring devices and uses are presented in Appendix D).

After the student decides how responses are to be measured (that is, after he structures the dependent variable), he should construct a graph that charts separate observations according to the independent variables of experimental interest. Thus, the total picture can be seen, and choices concerning the number of observations and treatments (manipulations) will be developed concurrently. The experimenter's time is almost always the determining factor; most experimental designs start out as good ten-year studies and become restricted to the time available. When the graph is constructed, simultaneous consideration of statistical tests will help structure the statistical evaluation.

STRUCTURING THE DESIGN

It is apparent that there is not a fixed hierarchy for designing an experiment. It is almost impossible even to get started without knowledge of all related aspects concerning experimentation. However, since the novice researcher has been introduced to many necessary concepts, procedures are now presented for structuring the composite design.

It is suggested that the investigator:

1. Review a great deal of experimental literature and evaluate published experiments on the basis of the criteria presented at the conclusion of Chapter Seven, pages 64–65.
2. Choose an area of investigation and delimit this area to a small topic while formulating appropriate hypotheses.
3. Go again to the literature and review all experiments that are related to the chosen topic.
4. Choose appropriate instrumentation for measuring observations (quantification). If appraisal instruments are not available, construct an objective measuring device that fits the topic (e.g., numerical rating scale).
5. If the topic does not generate its own experimental design, either (a) borrow a design that has previously been used in a similar experiment, or (b) study the Methods of Research Chart in Chapter Two; study Mill's canons in Chapter Six; study the Selected Research Designs and Statistical Tests chart, pp. 84–85; review statistical tests Chapter Nine, and then choose a composite design that fits the topic (e.g., two-sample independent—one-way analysis of variance).
6. Construct a graph that charts the number of separate observations on the

basis of the variables of experimental interest. For example, consider an experiment concerned with intonation: Title: "The Effect of Verbal Conditioning on Intonational Performance of College Vocalists." Hypothesis: Verbal conditioning will significantly improve performance as measured by the Stroboconn in plus and minus cent deviations from equal temperament. Total $N = 100$ subjects (randomly-selected sophomores) divided into an experimental group and a control group. Each subject performs on a pre-test (20 pitches) and a post-test (same 20 pitches). Therefore, total separate observations [pre-test $= (20 \times 50) + (20 \times 50)$] [post-test $= (20 \times 50) + (20 \times 50)$] $= 4,000$ pitches. If the total of separate observations gets too large, go back and limit some aspect(s) of the design to the point where the entire study can be accomplished in the time available.

7. Make sure that the methods of instrumentation and quantification, the methods of sampling and randomness, and the statistical test all are in harmony.

8. In a word, *control*. Be certain that the design is "tight" so that results can be interpreted on the basis of the intended design. Remember that *orders* of presentation need to be randomized unless you are specifically checking order effects. Often, there are many different randomizations in each simple experiment, for example, selection of subjects, assignment to pre-test, assignment to treatments, assignment to post-test, selection of pitches, presentation of pitches, etc. Initial rigor will insure greater scientific control. Start with an extremely simple topic and work for even greater refinement.

THE PROSPECTUS

If the experiment is conducted for a thesis or dissertation, a prospectus (proposal) is generally written prior to the investigation. It is advisable to write a prospectus regardless of whether or not it is required. The prospectus provides many benefits: (1) It necessitates a complete structural design before the collection of data; (2) it provides a sound basis for conducting the experiment without irrevocable mistakes; (3) if it is well written, it is substantially identical to the entire first part of the finished report and therefore the student has only to write the Results, Discussion, and Conclusion sections; and (4) it provides a contract that protects the student from inadequate research. If the student's prospectus is approved, the topic and methods of research are deemed appropriate. The prospectus can then be used as a basis for formal approval of the project in every respect. Undue stress on the student is greatly reduced by the writing and subsequent approval of a prospectus.

SCHOLARLY STYLE

Research is most often presented in what constitutes scholarly writing. Scholarly writing is unique, and most students have not had previous experience with this particular manner of expression. Scholarly research reporting is contrasted with essay style. The essay may analyze a problem, provide thoughtful inquiry and even possible solutions or points of view. The research report, on the other hand, constitutes an addition to knowledge and as such should present only the facts. The discussion section of the research report provides the scholar with a section intended to move beyond the limitations of the problem. However, it should also be written in scholarly style and not include personal conjecture that is not related to the general area of the experimental topic or the results.

Most papers written in scholarly style read as though they all could have been written by the same person. There is justification for this. The scholarly report should constitute the most objective presentation possible. Therefore, all attempts are made to discount the individual writing style of the researcher. When a scientist reads a research report, it is read for the scientific information it contains. While the reviewer is indeed concerned with *scientific opinions* of the researcher, he mainly desires concrete information based on the facts of the study, the researcher's experience in obtaining the results, and implications for further research. The scientist does not want to be entertained.

In scholarly writing, there should also be an "open-mindedness" that demonstrates a lack of absolutism or dogmatism. Hence, the researcher writes in the third person and refrains from the use of personal pronouns. The researcher most often "believes" in the results of his experiment, but does not make statements that might portray an opinionated disrespect for divergent points of view and additional research. Some research reports are immediately considered suspect because the writing style seems to betray a lack of objectivity, which indicates the researcher may have had such a preconceived bias that the experiment could not have demonstrated results contrary to these expectations. Research reporting should be free from ambiguity and be as concise as possible.

The student may practice scholarly writing by taking a paragraph of an essay or novel and rephrasing it to conform to scholarly style. For example, the phrase, "I want to know if practicing makes a difference in performance," might be phrased, "Differences concerning performance in relationship to practice will be assessed." The phrase, "I think practice helps performance," might be stated, "It would appear that practice improves performance." Scholarly style might seem both affected and cumbersome, yet the student needs to develop this technique. If the student begins writing without the use of I, he, she, you, and so on, most other conventions of scholarly writing will be forthcoming. Often, scholarly writing is not suitable in conveying or eliciting desired communication. Much of this text is written in essay style. However, research reports should conform to scholarly style, especially if a researcher wishes to have the formal report published.

THE FORMAL REPORT

Writing the formal research report is the final aspect of experimentation. After data have been gathered, classified, analyzed, and statistically evaluated, they constitute the raw material for the formal research report. There are many "models" for the research report, and the investigator is usually required by the institution in which he is studying to conform to the details of a prescribed style. Institutional and/or professional requirements must be checked for details of format. However, every report should include: (1) the problem, (2) the method, (3) the results, (4) a discussion of the results, and (5) a summary or abstract either at the beginning or the end, depending upon the style of the scientific area or prospective journal for publication.

The *title* of the report should be as succinct and informative as possible. Any investigator who has reviewed experimental literature knows how distressing it is to be misguided by an inappropriate title. Some research reports also include a brief summary of the entire study at the beginning. This is extremely beneficial to the reader and is recommended if it does not conflict with the specified format of the parent institution. The *introduction* section should provide an initiation into the topic, after which the *problem* should be presented with as much clarity as possible. Usually, *literature* is reviewed, *hypotheses* are stated, and *limitations and terminology* of the study are presented. Sometimes a *need for the study* section is also included. Clarity and good organization are imperative. It is sometimes suggested that the student outline each subject and paragraph before attempting to write the formal report.

The *method* section of the formal report constitutes the experimental design section. The student should have little difficulty with this section if the design has been well-constructed. The method section should be easily written using the step-by-step experimental procedures employed in the collection of data. All aspects of the design should be included.

The *results* section is the most informative section in the experimental report. Appropriate graphs and tables should be used to represent the results visually. Statistical tests need to be described and the original hypotheses either confirmed or rejected. The *discussion* section is the appropriate place for the experimenter to discuss the possible meaning and interpretation of the findings. Often, resultant information that was initially unexpected is provided by the study. Sometimes, the design does not prove adequate to test certain hypotheses of the topic. The investigator can then discuss these negative aspects with suggestions to further researchers. Implications of the study for other areas, and scientific opinions gained by the investigator, are presented in the discussion section. It is sometimes wise to inform the reader that this section does not constitute experimentally-tested hypotheses and therefore represents conjecture. The *conclusion* or *summary* section is usually extremely short and merely states the problem and lists the results of the *tested* hypotheses. Sometimes a *recommendations for further research* section is included.

CONCLUSION

This text is intended as an introduction to experimental research. Many musicians recognize the need for experimentation within the disciplines of music, but do not know how to get started. This text presumes to get the student started. Therefore, it is written specifically for the student. The sophisticated musician might find reasons for argument in Part One, the sophisticated researcher in Part Two.

The student is reminded that conjecture is conjecture regardless of intent or consequences. Some of the material included in the first five chapters is conjecture and should not be construed as representing experimental justification. It is presented to stimulate needed testing of various research topics.

This text has as an underlying theme the relation of an "either-or" attitude to many aspects of music and research. "Either-or" aspects of life need constant examination, leading toward greater discrimination. Some situations are definitely mutually exclusive, as with the control of an experiment where issues must be firmly differentiated. Conversely, many problems seem to arise because of an "either-or" attitude toward the many aspects of life that may be mutually reinforcing. Such is the case with music as an art and a science. Scientists are not necessarily insensitive; musicians are not necessarily non-thinking.

Another underlying aspect of "either-or" concerns the gradual process of inquiry toward greater knowledge and understanding. Man is often prone to extremes in this process and has a tendency both to magnify tentative results and to reject that which appears inconsequential. It is sometimes difficult to see the value of getting started, of adding a little to knowledge, of maintaining a quest for truth in the totality of ambiguity. Indeed, a tolerance for ambiguity seems essential in experimentation where one constantly strives to establish as much "truth" as possible, yet must be content with fragments of information and imperfect knowledge. Experimental research in music is at least one important event in life's greater sample space. If well done, it may prove extremely beneficial to the art of music. The researcher is challenged to deal with the acquisition of knowledge as a continuous process and seek to integrate the best from the past and present in order to develop capacity for that systematic and imaginative inquiry that extracts knowledge from information and wisdom from knowledge.

STUDY QUESTIONS

1. Summarize the steps to be taken in structuring an experimental design. What is the basic question regarding the relation of instrumentation to the design? Relate instrumentation with quantification.
2. What are some values derived from writing a prospectus?
3. Why are research reports written in scholarly style?
4. List and explain each of the parts of a formal report.
5. How is the "either-or" concept related to the gradual acquisition of knowledge in experimentation?

APPENDIX

A

selected periodicals

Acta Psychologia
Acta Psychotherapeutica et Psychosomatica
American Annals of the Deaf
American Archives of Rehabilitation Therapy
American Journal of Mental Deficiency
American Journal of Occupational Therapy
American Journal of Orthopsychiatry
American Journal of Physical Medicine
American Journal of Psychiatry
American Journal of Psychology
American Journal of Psychotherapy
American Journal of Sociology
American Music Teacher
American Psychologist
American Rehabilitation Committee, Bulletin
American Sociological Review
American String Teacher
Annales Medico-Psychologiques
Année Psychologique
Archives of Diseases of Children
Archives of General Psychiatry

Archives of Neurology
Archives of Otolaryngology
Archivio de Psicologia, Neurologia e Psichiatria
Arquivos Brasileiros de Psycotecnica

Behavioral Science
Behavior Research and Therapy
Brain
British Journal of Educational Psychology
British Journal of Psychology
British Medical Journal

California Journal of Educational Research
Cerebral Palsy Review
Child Development
Child Psychiatric Techniques
Child Welfare
Community Mental Health Journal
Comparative Psychiatry
Contemporary Psychology
Council for Research in Music Education
Crippled Child

Diseases of the Nervous System
Dissertation Abstracts

Education
Educational and Psychological Measurement
Elementary School Journal
Exceptional Children

Franklin Institute, Journal

Genetic Psychology Monographs
Gesundheit und Wohlfahrt
Gravesano Review

Hahinukh
Hinrichsen's Musical Yearbook

Instrumentalist
International Journal for the Education of the Blind
International Journal of Social Psychiatry

Journal de Psychologie Normale et Pathologique
Journal of Abnormal Psychology
Journal of Aesthetics and Art Criticism

Journal of American Medical Association
Journal of Applied Behavior Analysis
Journal of Applied Psychology
Journal of Clinical Psychology
Journal of Comparative Physiological Psychology
Journal of Consulting Psychology
Journal of Education
Journal of Educational Psychology
Journal of Educational Research
Journal of Experimental Child Psychology
Journal of Experimental Education
Journal of Experimental Psychology
Journal of General Psychology
Journal of Genetic Psychology
Journal of Heredity
Journal of Musicology
Journal of Music Therapy
Journal of Nervous and Mental Disease
Journal of Neurology and Psychiatry
Journal of Pediatrics
Journal of Personality
Journal of Personality and Social Psychology
Journal of Psychology
Journal of Rehabilitation
Journal of Research in Music Education
Journal of School Psychology
Journal of Social Issues
Journal of Social Psychology
Journal of Special Education
Journal of Speech and Hearing Disorders
Journal of the Acoustical Society of America
Journal of the American Musicological Society
Journal of the American Psychoanalytic Association

Lancet

Menninger Clinic Bulletin
Mental Health
Mental Hygiene
Mental Retardation
Merrill Palmer Quarterly
Music
Musical Courier
Music and Letters
Music Educators Journal (see also state publications, for example, *Florida Music
    Educator*)
Music Journal

Music News
Music Teachers National Association, Proceedings
Music Therapy, Yearbooks of the NAMT

National Association for Music Therapy, Bulletin
Nature
Neurology
New Biology

Occupational Therapy and Rehabilitation
Overture

Perceptual and Motor Skills
Personnel Psychology
Philips Technical Review
Plastic and Reconstructive Surgery
Psyche
Psychiatric Quarterly
Psychiatric Quarterly Supplement
Psychoanalytic Quarterly
Psychoanalytic Review
Psychologi
Psychological Abstracts
Psychological Bulletin
Psychological Monographs
Psychological Reports
Psychological Review
Psychology in the Schools
Psychology Today
Psychometrika

Quarterly Journal of Experimental Psychology

Recreation
Revista de Psicologia General y Aplicada
Revue Belge de Psychologie et de Pédagogie

School Musician
Schweitzer Archiv für Neurologie, Neurochirurgie und Psychiatrie
Science
Scientific Monthly
See and Hear
Social Forces
Sound
Spastics Quarterly
State medical journals (Pennsylvania, New York, West Virginia, etc.)

Teachers College Record: Columbia University
Today's Health
Tohoku Psychologica Folia

Volta Review
Voprosy Psikhologii

Yearbook of Psychoanalysis
Young Children

Zeitschrift für Experimentelle und Angewandte Psychologie
Zeitschrift für Psychotherapie und Medizinische Psychologie

APPENDIX
B

selected statistical references

Self-instruction in statistics is not preferred and, in fact, should be discouraged. Nevertheless, the following texts will provide a complete background in statistics *if* the texts are studied and used in the order indicated.

1. Huff, Darrell. *How to Lie with Statistics*. New York: W.W. Norton & Company, Inc., 1954. Excellent first book to be read before any elementary texts. Contains humorous examples of deceptive statistical tricks. Read seriously, it prevents later errors of similar kind.

2. McCullough, H., and Celeste and Loche Van Atta. *Statistical Concepts: A Program for Self Instruction*. New York: McGraw-Hill Book Company, 1963.

3. Siegel, Sidney. *Nonparametric Statistics for the Behavioral Sciences*. New York: McGraw-Hill Book Company, 1956. Easily-understood text. Best available source for the use of nonparametric statistics (twenty-seven nonparametrics techniques with examples). Includes step-by-step calculation procedures and can be read without prior experience in statistics.

4. Edwards, Allen, L. *Statistical Analysis*. New York: Holt, Rinehart & Winston, 1958. Excellent text for beginners. Covers *t* tests, analysis of variance, and correlation coefficients.

5. Hays, William L. *Statistics for Psychologists*. New York: Holt, Rinehart &

Winston, 1963. Text builds from a basis of set theory and covers all common parametric statistics, gives some experimental design as well as some nonparametrics. Considered by many the best available text for elementary and advanced statistics.

6. Winer, B.F. *Statistical Principles in Experimental Design*. New York: Mc-Graw-Hill Book Company, 1962. Most comprehensive advanced source for experimental design. Includes many model designs and all appropriate tables, but should not be consulted without a statistician's aid or prior experience.

7. Lindgren, B.W. *Statistical Theory*. New York: The Macmillan Company, 1962. Highly advanced text in statistical theory. Should not be read without advanced mathematical background.

APPENDIX
C

glossary of statistical terms and tests

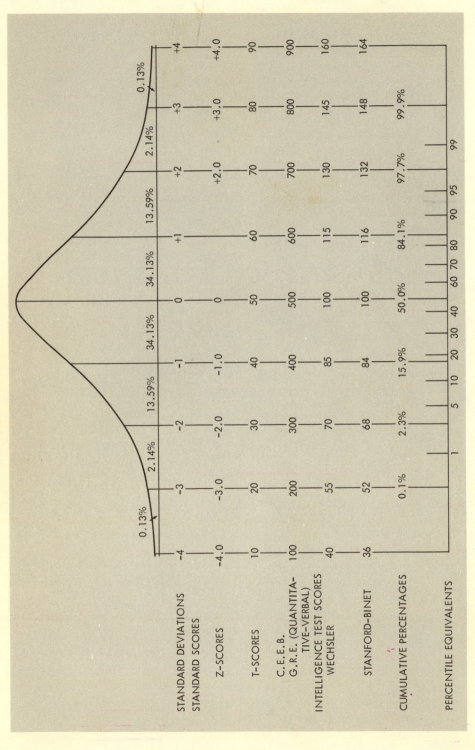

NORMAL CURVE WITH APPROXIMATIONS AMONG DERIVED SCORES

Analysis of Covariance — Original data on a variable of experimental interest are adjusted on the basis of known pre-experimental differences as measured on some other variable. This analysis permits elimination of that part of the variability accounted for by pre-experimental differences. Any bias in apparent experimental manipulation can thereby be reduced to a greater extent than when randomization is used. (*See:* Winer, *Statistical Principles in Experimental Design,* pp. 578–618.)

Analysis of Variance (one-way) — One of two basic designs for comparing groups of subjects after experimental manipulation. Analysis of variance involves three or more *independent* random samples, not necessarily of the same size. The test compares experimental group means. (*See:* Edwards, *Statistical Analysis,* pp. 141–47.)

Analysis of Variance (two-way) — Another basic design (see above) for comparing three or more groups on two separate variables simultaneously. The same individuals, cases, or groups are compared under both conditions. The tests compares differences in means. (*See:* Edwards, pp. 141–47.)

Arithmetic Mean—Mean—Generally called the "average," except in statistics. The mean is equal to the sum of the scores divided by the total number of scores. Computational symbols: $\frac{\Sigma X}{N} = \bar{X}$ ($\bar{X}$ = arithmetic mean). Σ = Greek capital letter sigma used to indicate the "sum of a series of measures." X = a raw score (your data) in a series of measures. ΣX = the sum of all the measures adding the measures with a cumulative total. N = the number of measures (total number of observations taken in a particular series).

Chi Square (χ^2) Used when measurements are classified in frequencies, i.e., when the number of subjects who fall into two or more categories is the basic data. The question to be answered is whether or not the frequencies observed in the categories are significantly different from some expected frequencies. The expected frequencies are normally derived from the null hypothesis. Formula: $\chi^2 = \Sigma \frac{(O - E)^2}{E}$. O = observed frequency. E = corresponding expected frequencies. After computation, degrees of freedom are used in consultation with χ^2 Table. (*See:* One-sample χ^2, Siegel, *Non-parametric Statistics for the Behavioral Sciences,* pp. 42–47; Two-sample χ^2, Siegel, pp. 104–11; χ^2 for independent samples, Siegel, pp. 175–79).

Cochran Q Test — A method for testing whether three or more matched sets of frequencies or proportions differ significantly among themselves. (*See:* Siegel, pp. 161–66.)

Confounding — Concurrent changing of two or more variables. Thus, results cannot be said to be attributed to a single variable.

Control Group — Ideally, this is a group which is like the experimental group in every way that would affect the outcome of the experiment, except for one manipulated variable.

Correlation — The interrelation between two or more conditions or events. Correlations are generally used when variables under study cannot be experimentally controlled. Correlations never indicate causality and rarely even indicate whether either variable is influencing the other. Correlations are measures of relationships and are expressed as positive, negative, or zero correlations. A positive correlation exists when scores tend to be the same on both variables. A negative correlation exists when low scores on one variable are associated with high scores on another variable. A zero correlation exists when there is little or no relationship between the scores on two variables.

Dependent Variable — The phenomenon that appears, disappears, or changes when the independent variable is applied, removed, or varied. The dependent measure is usually the test score.

Descriptive Statistics — Characteristics of a set of scores given in statistical terms. Descriptive statistics are used to describe rather than to predict.

Element of a Sample — Each entity or thing within a collection of things, grouped together on any basis, is termed an element of that collection. The assumption exists that states that each individual element of a sample can be distinguished from every other element.

Empirical — Methods based entirely upon experimentation and observations.

Equivalent-Sample Technique — A method of "matching" to overcome the difficulty that results because extraneous differences exist between groups of experimental subjects. Thus, the samples studied are related before the fact. Matching may best be achieved by using each subject as his own control, but many experiments pair subjects and then assign the two members of each pair to two different experimental conditions.

Experimental Group — The experimental group for which the experimenter attempts to hold constant all but one of the factors that might affect the outcome of the experiment, or the group or groups to which particular treatments are applied.

Experimental Variables — Any variables that can be manipulated or varied in accordance with the demands of the experimenter.

Fisher Exact Probability Test — An exact probability test used with small sample size to test differences between samples on the basis of central tendency. (*See:* Siegel, pp. 96–104.)

Friedman Two-Way Analysis of Variance by Rank—Can be used to test the hypothesis that two or more samples have been drawn from the same population. Data from the matched samples must be in at least an ordinal scale. (*See:* Siegel, pp. 166–72.)

Homogeneous — Composed of similar or identical elements or parts; uniform.

Independence of Observation — Independence indicates that each observation is not influenced by other observations. Some statistical tests are used to test for independence of observations.

Independent Groups — Different groups of subjects selected separately. An experiment that uses different groups of subjects for each condition of the experiment is based on independent groups.

Independent Variable — The factor purposively manipulated to ascertain its relationship with the dependent variable. Sometimes thought of as the "cause" of the dependent measure of "effect."

Inferential Statistics — The procedure whereby descriptive statistics are used to make predictions in either of two general ways: (1) The concept of reliability can be viewed as a prediction that what once was is still the same; (2) more sophisticated types of prediction are those in which descriptions at a given time and under certain conditions are used to guess (predict) what the descriptions will be at a later time and under slightly different conditions.

Interactions in Analysis of Variance — The use of two variables in the same experiment permits the assessment of any effects of either variable on a measured outcome. In addition, it is possible to gain information about the *combined* effects of both variables. When interactions between variables are discovered, the resulting outcome is better predicted by using such information than by using information about each variable separately.

Kendall's Tau — A measure of relationship between two sets of ranked numbers. This correlation is based on a probability analysis of all possible rank orders and the probability of the ranks reversing relative positions on two different rank-order scales. (*See:* Siegel, pp. 213–29; Hays, pp. 647–55.)

Kolmogorov-Smirnov One-Sample Test — A "goodness of fit" test for ranked data. (*See:* Siegel, pp. 47–52.)

Kolmogorov-Smirnov Two-Sample Test — A test of significance for two independent samples. (*See:* Siegel, pp. 127–36.)

Kruskal-Wallis One-Way Analysis of Variance by Ranks — A useful test for deciding whether two or more independent samples are from different populations. (*See:* Siegel, pp. 184–93.)

Mann-Whitney U — With ordinal measurement the Mann-Whitney *U* is used to determine whether two independent groups have been drawn from the same population. This test is an alternative to the parametric *t* test. (*See:* Siegel, pp. 116–27.)

McNemar Test for the Significance of Changes — This test is applicable to designs where persons are used as their own controls. Measurement should be of either a nominal or an ordinal scale. (*See:* Siegel, pp. 63–67.)

Median — Another label for the fiftieth percentile. The point above which 50% of the cases fall and below which 50% of the cases fall.

Mode — The score that occurs most frequently in a series of scores.

Null Hypothesis — The assumption that there is no difference between the population measured and the value under test. The null hypothesis is usually formulated for the express purpose of being rejected, in which case the alternative hypothesis may be accepted.

One-Sample Technique — One-sample techniques usually involve drawing on a random sample and testing whether or not the sample was drawn from a parent population with any hypothesized distribution. A common technique is to assess the difference between an observed (sample) mean and the expected (population) mean through the use of a *t* test. (*See:* Edwards, pp. 126–33). Non-parametric tests are also available. (*See:* Siegel, pp. 36–38.)

Pearson's Product-Moment Correlation — A method to determine whether or not some observed association in a sample of scores indicates that the variables under study are most probably associated in the population from which the sample was drawn. The Pearson *r* requires scores that represent measurement in at least an equal-interval scale. The value of the Pearson *r* is actually equal to the average of the *z*-score products for the two pairs. (*See:* Hays, *Statistics for Psychologists,* pp. 493–538.)

Percentile — The percentile rank of any specific score is a value indicating the percent of cases in a distribution falling at or below this score.

Pre-Written Statistical Programs — Many universities have computer programs which can be used by persons who have no knowledge of computer programming (often called "canned programs"). The particular programs are pre-written and it is only necessary to know how to "plug-in" to the program. Consult your nearest computer center for this service.

Probability — The probability that any event will occur is generally expressed as a number from 0 to 1.00. Two methods are used: (1) The *relative frequency* method compares the occurrence of an event over some number of occasions on which the event could have occurred. This proportion is said to be equal to the probability of the event; (2) the *mathematical limits* method requires that one make certain mathematical assumptions that allow one to describe the relative frequency of the event in question, by means of an equation. If it can be shown that this relative frequency value approaches some stable value (limit) as the number of trials approaches infinity, then this limiting value of the relative frequency of an event is defined as the probability of the event.

Proposition — A fundamental assumption not meant to be tested, such as a statement concerning empirical observations. A set of propositions is often used within a given logical framework to yield further propositions implied by the original set. The further propositions (theorems) derived will depend upon the rules for deduction as well as upon original statements. Propositions may be tested indirectly by observing the concurrence or lack of it between theorems and observations.

Reliability — The degree to which one obtains the same result with a measuring device when the same variable is measured twice (or more).

Sample Size — Dependent upon the experimental design and the purposes of the experiment. Formulas can also be used to determine the sample size. (*See:* Hays, p. 204–6.)

Sets — Any collection of things grouped together for any reason may be called a set. Each entity or thing within such a collection will be termed an element or member of that set. It is assumed that each element or member of a set can be distinguished from every other element.

Sign Test — This test uses plus and minus signs rather than any other kind of measurement. The test emphasizes direction of difference between two scores or series of matched scores. The idea is to find if the conditions are different (for example, before and after experimental treatment). (*See:* Siegel, pp. 68–75.)

Spearman Rank Correlation Coefficient — A measurement of association requiring that both variables be measured in at least an ordinal scale. Objects or individuals under study may be ranked in two ordered series. This statistic is called rho. (*See:* Siegel, pp. 202–13).

Standard Deviation — An average of deviation scores or the root mean square deviation. A particular type of average wherein all scores are taken into consideration. Standard Deviation is a statistic that describes variability of measures. Generally, it is a figure that represents overall about one-sixth of the total range of a group of scores.

Calculation:

1. Find the mean (X) by summing all the raw scores and dividing by the total number of scores (N).
2. Subtract the mean from each raw score and square each result = $(X - X)^2$.
3. Sum the squares (Σx^2).
4. Divide the sum by the total observations minus one (N-1).
5. Take the square root of this figure.

Therefore, standard deviation $= \sqrt{\dfrac{\Sigma x^2}{N}}$.

Standard Score (z score) — A value that indicates the amount by which a raw score deviates from the mean $(\overline{X})$ in standard deviation units. z scores from different distributions of scores are directly comparable. If the raw score is below the mean $(\overline{X})$ the z score is given a minus value. z scores normally range from −3.00 to +3.00 (6 standard deviation units). When a raw score equals the mean, z = 0.

A T score is another form of standard score. T scores avoid the use of negative numbers by placing the mean raw scores equal to a T score of 50 and equating the raw score standard deviation to 10 T-score points. Thus, a score 1 standard deviation above the mean (z score of 1) would have a T score of 60, that is, 50 + 10. A score 1 standard deviation below the mean (a z score of −1) would have a T score of 40.

t-Test — Used to statistically compare differences between means. The *t*-test is essentially a z score and actually shows the number of deviation units from a mean. (*See:* Edwards, pp. 126–33.)

Trend Studies — A study designed to assess the difference between groups over time when subjected to a series of experiences or manipulations.

Validity — The degree to which a test actually measures what it purports to measure. The determination of validity requires independent external *criteria* of whatever the test is designed to measure.

Variability — The extent of individual differences around the central tendency of a group of scores, the central tendency being a measure that provides a single, most typical, or representative score to characterize the performance of the entire group. Variability may be reported in terms of the *range* between the highest and lowest scores, the deviation of each individual score from the mean of the group, the *standard deviation,* or the *variance* or *mean square deviation.*

Variance (Equal to the Standard Deviation Squared) — This is generally called the mean square rather than the variance especially when dealing with analysis of variance routines. An excellent measure of variability both within a single series and for comparing one distribution with another.

Wilcoxen Matched Pairs Signed Rank Test — A test that utilizes information concerning both the direction of the differences within pairs and the magnitude of that difference. (*See:* Siegel, pp. 75–83.)

APPENDIX
D

equipment descriptions

The following equipment has been found useful for many experiments in music. The beginning researcher should be aware of the importance of precise instrumentation. However, he should realize that many experiments can be conducted with resourceful use of equipment at his disposal.

CATHODE-RAY OSCILLOSCOPE

The oscilloscope is used to obtain a picture of the wave form of a circuit. Controls on the oscilloscope enable the experimenter to view a constantly changing signal as if it were drawn on graph paper. From the display, the wave form can be evaluated in terms of time and amplitude characteristics. Resultant wave forms can be compared (matched) when used in conjunction with an overlay pattern; when the overlay is affixed to the screen of the oscilloscope comparative analyses can be drawn.

When used in conjunction with a microphone and an amplifier, the oscilloscope can be used to display various vocal patterns, i.e., differentiation of vowel sounds and the individual wave patterns produced on various musical instruments. Connect the microphone to the input of the amplifier and the output of the amplifier to the vertical input of the oscilloscope. This instrumentation suggests investigation into the areas of speech and instrumental techniques of tone production.

The oscilloscope not only is a valuable tool in the measurement of signal voltages; but as a read-out and visual monitoring device it provides versatile application in the field of research. Additional utilization of the instrument will become apparent to the experimenter as he proceeds into the area of testing and measurements.

ELECTRONIC SWITCH

The Electronic Switch serves as an accessory to be used in combination with the oscilloscope. It enables the experimenter to view two signals at the same time on the screen of the scope. Separate positioning controls are provided to superimpose or separate the signals for comparative analysis or individual observation. Additional controls include: separate gain controls for each channel, variable switching rate control, and a synchronous output control, which locks the scope sweep to the signal output of the switch. A typical example of its use is to simultaneously observe a signal before and after any additional modulation or modification takes place, i.e., viewing the wave form of a signal as it appears at both the input and output stages of an amplifier.

AUDIO GENERATOR

The audio generator can provide signal sources of known frequency, form, and amplitude. Some generators produce both sine and square waves, which may be viewed separately or simultaneously on an oscilloscope without affecting either wave form. Typical laboratory application of the instrument would include using the generator as an audiometer, i.e., testing the frequency and threshold responses of subjects. In testing for pitch discrimination, it would be advisable to obtain an instrument that provides a continuous (sweep) coverage from 10 cps — 20 kc. A metered output, calibrated in volts and decibels, is available on some instruments, from which frequency response curves can be established.

D.C. POWER SUPPLY

The D.C. power supply has numerous applications in the laboratory, especially where a source of variable, low-power, filtered, D.C. voltage is required. Specifications should include: a rated fused output of at least 1 ampere and a variable voltage output from 0 — 48 volts. Most instruments provide a continuously metered output of voltage and current.

MULTIMETER — VACUUM TUBE VOLTMETER

The multimeter or volt-ohmmeter provides wide voltage, current, and resistance measurements. The VOM is self-powered, providing portable use in the design and repair of electronic equipment. Occasionally, it becomes necessary to perform voltage checks on equipment without disturbing the electrical characteristics of a particular circuit. Under these conditions, use a vacuum tube voltmeter. The vtvm draws so little current from the circuit that the resultant voltage drop becomes negligible.

Capacitance—Resistance Decades

Capacitance and resistance decades provide convenient switch-selection of desired capacitance or resistance values in a circuit. The decades can be used to show effects of different capacitance or resistance values on circuit operation, and in servicing to estimate proper values for component replacement in "burned-out" circuitry.

Electric Chronoscope

The chronoscope is essentially a motor-driven electric clock with a sweep-1/100-second hand. It provides a convenient measurement of "on-task" time intervals during a "trial" period. The clock may be started and stopped mechanically or electrically. It records in seconds and hundredths of a second.

Pulse-Activated Switch

The pulse-activated switch, when used in conjunction with a microphone or tape recorder, can provide reliable and instantaneous "on" and "off" switching of an electrical circuit. A typical use of the switch is to activate the electric clutch (on time-recording devices) upon commencement of a sound or electronic impulse. The switch may also be touch-activated. A variable sensitivity control is usually provided on the instrument.

Stroboscope (Stroboconn-Strobotuner)

The stroboscope is designed to detect variances in pitch. It is tuned to A-440 cps. A strobe-light is modulated by the pitch of the sound produced and is focused on rotating discs, markings on which seemingly move forward or backward depending on sharpness or flatness of the note produced. A control knob is provided to stop the motion of the markings, at which time a direct reading is available in "cents" sharp or flat from exact pitch; a cent is 1/100 of a semi-tone (C.G. Conn, Ltd., Elkhart, Indiana).

Tempo/Tuner

The tempo/tuner is a small battery operated instrument designed as a combination metronome/audio generator. Because of its small size and portability, it is an ideal instrument for many simple experiments. (Model W2-1000, Electronic Research Products, Los Altos, California, distributed by Selmer, Elkhart, Indiana.)

Johnson Intonation Trainer

The Johnson Intonation Trainer is a portable electronic keyboard instrument with *adjustable* tuning for the twelve tones of the chromatic scale. It has a three octave keyboard and four possible timbres. The adjustable tuning (each of the 37 tones has a tunable range of about six semitones) makes this an excellent instrument for many possible experiments in perception as well as in educational research (E.F. Johnson Company, Waseca, Minnesota).

ADDITIONAL EQUIPMENT

4-Track Stereo Tape Recorder w/microphones, separate record/playback heads
Stereo phonograph w/integrated stereo amplifier system
Tuning forks, A = 440, B = 466.16, C = 261.63
Variac Transformer (variable A.C. power supply)

Soldering gun (medium duty)
Roll resin flux core solder—60/40 alloy
Multi-purpose screwdriver set—slotted and Phillips
Hollow-shaft nutdriver set ($\frac{1}{16}$"–$\frac{3}{8}$")
Combination pliers
Diagonal cutters—$4\frac{1}{2}$"
Long nose pliers—6"
Wire stripper
Lock pliers
Hammer—16 oz. head
Hacksaw
Hand-reamer—$\frac{1}{8}$" point
Center punch
Adjustable wrench—6"
Hand drill
Drill set—$\frac{1}{16}$"–$\frac{1}{4}$"
Tool box
High-intensity lamp
Magnifying glass
Vise—medium size
Rubber floor strip—3' wide, length to suit (minimizes shock hazard when using electrical equipment)

Resistor assortment, 1 watt
Resistor assortment, 5–15 watts
Capacitor assortment—600 volt rating
Electrolytic capacitor assortment—450 volt rating
Hook-up wire assortment
Tube socket assortment (octals—7- and 9-pin types)
Assorted hardware—nuts, screws, washers, etc.
Digital counter, 110 VAC, pulse-activated
Digital counter, 12-24 VDC, pulse-activated
Toggle switch assortment, SPST, SPDT, DPST, DPDT, etc.
Binding post assortment, red and black
Pushbutton switch assortment, SPST
Indicator lamp, socket, and jewel assortment
Time-delay relay, adjustable 1-10 sec., DPDT, 10 amp. rated

For additional information about electrical instrumentation see: Cornswett, Tom N., *The Design of Electric Circuits in the Behavioral Sciences* (New York: Wiley and Sons, Inc., 1963).

Electronic Equipment and Parts Catalogues:

Allied Electronics
100 N. Western Avenue, Chicago, Illinois 60680

Lafayette Radio Electronics
111 Jericho Turnpike, Syosset, L. I. New York 11791

Radio Shack Corporation
730 Commonwealth Avenue, Boston, Massachusetts 02215

KITS

Heathkit Electronics
3462–66 W. Devon Avenue, Chicago, Illinois 60680

Eico Electronic Instrument Company, Inc.
131–01 39th Avenue, Flushing, New York 11352

index